A HARV

PEACE

A HARVEST OF PEACE

Tools to Cultivate the Fruit of the Spirit

REBEKAH MONTGOMERY

ISBN 1-57748-844-X

Unless otherwise noted, all Scripture quotations are taken from the King James Version of the Bible.

Scriptures marked NIV are taken from the *Holy Bible: New International Version*®. NIV®. Copyright © 1973, 1978, 1984 by International Bible Society. Used by permission of Zondervan Publishing House.

Scripture quotations marked NKJV are taken from the New King James Version. Copyright © 1979, 1980, 1982 by Thomas Nelson, Inc. Used by permission. All rights reserved.

Published by Promise Press, an imprint of Barbour Publishing, Inc., P.O. Box 719, Uhrichsville, Ohio 44683
www.barbourbooks.com

Printed in the United States of America.

Dedication

To my brothers,
Victor, Dave, Jonathan, Steve, Tim, and Mark;
my dad, Carl V. Binkley;
and my other dad, John B.

Throughout this book,
names have been changed to
protect the privacy of individuals.

Chapter 1

God's Divine Peace:
What Is It?

Do not be anxious about anything,
but in everything, by prayer and petition,
with thanksgiving, present your requests to God.
And the peace of God,
which transcends all understanding,
will guard your hearts and your minds in Christ Jesus.
PHILIPPIANS 4:6–7 NIV

Inner peace is
a difficult concept to define,
but it is easy to identify its absence.
Like joy, it goes beyond mere emotion.
And it certainly
transcends circumstance.
Peace is
the ability to lie in bed at night,
look up at the ceiling,
and know everything is going to be
all right when
everything really isn't all right.
Peace is an inner settledness.

CHARLES STANLEY

The supernatural peace of God is a curious peace. It appears during the wild and windy storms of life. It thrives on the precipices of faith. It bears fruit when savage trials corner believers, threatening to devour them. In these moments of tribulation, those who flee to the shadow of the Almighty find He is the Rock in a weary land, the Shelter in the time of storm, the Cleft in the rock, the all-sufficient One, the Comforter, the Great Physician, the Prince of Peace.

God's peace is. . .

- comfort when you are grieving.
- shelter beneath His wings.
- shade in a spiritual desert.
- safety when you're threatened.
- forgiveness when you've erred.
- security in the face of danger.
- knowing you have a home in heaven.
- having freedom in your soul even if your body is imprisoned.
- liberation from a sinful past.
- accepting God's forgiveness.
- *knowing Jesus.*

We find God's peace in. . .

- learning the promises of His Word, the Bible.
- believing His promises are true.
- trusting that God loves us.
- unconditionally accepting His will for our lives.
- continuing to trust Him regardless of our circumstances.
- accepting God's forgiveness for our sins.
- crowning Jesus Lord of our lives.
- *knowing Jesus.*

Witnesses of God's Peace

Life is tough. It often seems cruel, capricious, and unfair. Yet in the midst of all that life throws at you, God can give you His supernatural peace. When God gives supernatural peace, it doesn't mean that you will float away on a pink cloud or that all of your teardrops will magically transform into butterflies. It does mean that God walks beside you through the storms of life—and even if the storm is caused by your own sin and disobedience, God still extends His nail-pierced hand to you.

In His hand, you'll find His strength, comfort, healing,

help, wisdom, and courage. Take His hand, as did these people, and find peace in His presence.

"When I was in college and unmarried," said Kelly, "I got pregnant and aborted a baby. At the time, I knew my lifestyle was wrong, and I knew it was murder to have an abortion, but I did it anyway.

"I was okay until I gave birth to another child, my daughter, and then I realized what I had done—I was responsible for the death of my own child. I was haunted by what I had done. I tried everything—counseling, talking to pastors, apologizing to my unborn baby—but nothing gave me peace until I confessed my sin to God and asked Him for forgiveness.

"It sounds simple. . .but it took me a long time before I could believe that God would forgive me. My sin was against Him as well as my unborn child. I can't bring back my lost baby. Nothing will change that, but I am free from the guilt. I have peace because God has forgiven me."

"I raised my children to know God," said Cynthia, "but all three have chosen to go their own ways. Naturally, I'm devastated they have all turned their backs on the Lord, but I don't feel like the situation is hopeless. I raised them right; I have faith in the upbringing I gave them. I believe the Bible when it says if we raise up children in the way they should go, they will not depart from it. But even more than that, I have peace because on a daily basis, I bring my children before the throne of the Almighty. I pray for His protection over them and His intervention in their lives. I trust Him, and while the way they live grieves me, I have peace that God will bring them back to Himself."

"I worked for that company for thirty-two years," said Herb. "I would have had three more years until I could have retired with full benefits. Of course I'm unhappy that they declared bankruptcy, but God hasn't gone out of business. He's in control.

"It would be a lie to say I'm not uneasy, because I am. There is something about the unknown that makes a person a little nervous, but that's not to say I don't trust God. I know He's doing something. I'm in a state of alert, a listening-for-His-voice phase.

"I don't know what He's going to do with my life. I still have kids in college and my wife to support. But God knows my needs. I've asked Him for help. I can trust Him to take care of me."

"When my wife left me and took the boys," said Nick, "I went into shock for a while. I didn't know where she was, and I couldn't believe she was gone. I still don't have a satisfactory answer as to why she left me. I know I did some things wrong in our marriage, but I didn't think it was as bad as all that!

"At first, I was mad at God, mad at her, mad at her parents, mad at the whole world. After a while, when I realized that it wasn't God's fault, I started going back to church, reading my Bible, and praying.

"God knows I'm a married kind of guy; He knows I don't want to spend my life alone and without my sons. I used to tell God what I wanted Him to do about this situation—and then I'd be frustrated because He didn't handle things the way I told Him. Now I ask Him, instead, what He wants me to do about the situation. Sometimes, I sense God saying, 'Call her and just talk. Or better yet, don't talk, listen!' Sometimes, He says, 'Don't do anything,' and I don't like that, but I've found out the hard way that it's better if I listen to Him and not run ahead of His will.

"I don't know how this situation with my wife and kids will turn out, but I've got a peace about it. That doesn't mean God is going to do what I want—I know better—but it means God is in control. He'll eventually work it out for good. Sometimes that's hard for me to accept—but when I just trust Him, I am peaceful."

"I know God called me to be a missionary," Lori said, "but I have to raise all of this support money to go. When the mission organization first told me how much money I had to have pledged, I thought, *No way!* But little by little, God has supplied. I'm not sure how He'll do it, but I have a peace that God will pull all of the pledges together. It's actually kind of fun to watch where all of the money comes from!"

God Speaks Peace in the Language of Your Soul

- For those who are exhausted, like Elijah, God comforts in a still, small voice.
- For those who are insecure, like Moses, God directs from a burning bush.
- For those who are angry, like Saul of Tarsus, God knocks them to the ground and speaks like thunder.
- For those who are willing, like Jesus, God sends a dove to pronounce a blessing.
- For those who are confused, like Jacob, God extends a ladder from heaven to show His accompanying power.
- For those who are in harm's way, like Lot and his family, God sends angels to give direction.
- For those who are persecuted, like Joseph, God sends dreams to encourage.
- For those who need deliverance, like Moses and the children of Israel, God sends a strong wind to part the sea.

- For those who need safe passage, like Jesus and the disciples, God calms the sea.
- For those who are in need, like the Israelites in the wilderness, God sends manna.
- For those driven mad by the conflicts of life, like King Saul, God sends the comfort of the Psalms.
- For those who are imprisoned, like Paul and Silas, God sends a song in the night.

Whoever you are, whatever your need, God speaks peace in the language of your soul.

Brother Lawrence's Prayer for Peace

"I know not what I shall become; it seems to me that peace of soul and repose of spirit descend on me, even in sleep. To be without the sense of this peace, would be affliction indeed. . . .

"I know not what God purposes with me, or keeps me for; I am in a calm so great that I fear naught. What can I fear, when I am with Him; and with Him, in His Presence, I hold myself the most I can. May all things praise Him. Amen."

The Voice of God over the Storm

If you want to further your public career—or at very minimum keep your head firmly attached to your shoulders—one way NOT to do that is to arouse the wrath of a bloodythirsty queen with an overdeveloped sense of vengeance. Jezebel didn't like Elijah, a prophet of God, in the first place. He reminded her subjects of the God of Abraham, Isaac, and Jacob. She was trying to wipe out all memory of Him and unite the country behind the worship of her gods, Asherah and Baal. But Jezebel favored Elijah much less now that he had caused all her prophets, 850 of them, to be wiped out in one swoop. Upon hearing this news, she had thundered and raged, then sent Elijah a message: "May the gods deal with me, be it ever so severely, if by this time tomorrow I do not make you like that of one of my priests!"

Dead, in other words.

Typically, Elijah wasn't the sort of person to panic. An athletic man's man, he stood toe-to-toe with the best of warriors. But dealing with Jezebel was something entirely different. While she was immoral and totally ruthless, she was also beautiful, persuasive, and fascinating. For the moment, Israel was hers. Not only did she lead her husband, King Ahab, around by the nose like he was a love-struck bull; the entire nation had fallen under her charismatic spell. The army was at her disposal and whim. And Jezebel had spies everywhere. The most innocent-appearing child, the most innocuous-looking woman, the old beggar man, all could be in her employ. There was no safe place to hide in the entire country.

Now she had set her sights on Elijah; he was definitely in her crosshairs. She had publicly sworn an oath, and all of her considerable resources were dedicated to his capture and demise.

So Elijah ran for his life. Hoping to throw his pursuer off his trail, he crossed the border into Judah and left his servant behind in Beersheba. Alone, he could travel faster and with more security. Then he headed south for the desert where the sands shifted moment by moment. A man's footprints disappeared as he made them. In a swirling gust, a huge mountain could be transported miles away grain by grain. With no food or water available from the land, it was a good, albeit dangerous, place to hide. For forty days, Elijah pushed himself forward through the sand, safe from Jezebel's long reach, now pursued only by the ghosts of his own fears.

It is often in the lonely moments that we are tempted to lie to ourselves. We don't need Satan in the guise of a serpent to hiss half-truths into our ears; we tell them to ourselves. So it was with Elijah. He had seen the tomb of another lonely pilgrim, the patriarch Abraham, in Beersheba; it was filled with bones. But Elijah badly needed a word from Jehovah, the God of the living. Hoping, listening on the wind, he headed for Mount Horeb (also known as Mount Sinai), the mountain of God. Here is where the hand of God chiseled out stone tablets and wrote His Law upon them. Perhaps here God would reveal Himself to him and tell him what to do.

As he trudged mile after mile over undulating sand and scaled rocky slopes, never seeing another living soul or even sighting a bird or animal, he felt his dedication to God to be unique in all the universe. He was solitary: the last man of God anywhere. He would go back to the advent of Israel's covenant with God and wait for an answer from Him. Or die alone.

He found a cave in the heart of the mountain and slept. As the new day dawned, Elijah heard the voice of God.

"What are you doing here, Elijah?" God asked him. With a pout of self-pity in his voice, he replied, "I have been very zealous for the LORD God Almighty. The Israelites have rejected Your covenant, broken down Your altars; and put Your prophets to death with the sword. I am the only one left, and now they are trying to kill me, too."

The LORD said, "Go out and stand on the mountain in the presence of the LORD, for the LORD is about to pass by."

Elijah crept out of the cave. Over the summit, a sickly, greenish band of sky peeked out from under a row of angry, rolling clouds. Then, like the finger of God's judgment, a funnel cloud dropped out of the sky and struck the mountains with an unbridled surge of wind power. Boulders split and careened wildly down the peaks. Entire cliff faces were sliced off, and with a shuddering moan, cartwheeled into deep ravines. Elijah crouched against the breast of this mountain to which he had run for refuge, trembling in awe. Even the mountain of God was feeble when pitted against His very power! As the wind howled and moaned, Elijah listened for the voice of God, straining for a word even as the clouds retreated into the heavens. But God was silent.

Elijah waited, searching the sky to see if God would send lightning to write His instructions upon the ruined heights. But as he waited in the stillness after the storm, leaning against the mountain, he sensed a slight tremor. It was more like a small vibration, the distant throbbing of a faint pulse. It grew beneath his hands and under his feet until it seemed that the heart of the mountain was breaking. What caves and hiding places the storm had spared were now shattered, crumbled, and destroyed. There was no safe place on the mountain or within it. Elijah clung to the rocks for support, but they seemed ready to throw off his hands and hurl him into nothingness. Then, after a few final heaving groans, the rocking ceased.

Again, Elijah waited, listening, straining to hear the voice who commanded everything from the wind of the heavens to the entrails of the earth. But God was silent.

Then he heard faint crackling, a dry rustling of the desert-seared grasses, and a sighing wind. Straining to see the summit and ascertain what was descending upon him from the heights, he noticed several poisonous adders slithering rapidly along the ground, heads up, racing for the lowland. His first thought was to club them in self-defense; but they took no heed of him nor did they take note of the mice that ran through their midst, scampering over their coiled scales as if they were no threat to them. Behind them came rabbit and fox together, deer and wolf, wild goats and mountain lion—all ignoring their age-long enmity in a headlong rush to escape the encroaching flames. The fire swept down the mountainside consuming everything living in its path. When it passed, only Elijah remained. A breeze stirred up the gray ashes and Elijah listened. But God was silent.

Elijah was now truly alone. The mountain was utterly destroyed. No shelter but his cave, no animals, not even a scrap of vegetation remained. There was only Elijah.

And God. After the noise, the destruction, the awful violence, Elijah strained to hear His voice. He waited patiently, composing his heart, ready to hear whatever God would say to him. Then, in a gentle whisper, God called to him. Elijah covered his face, standing again at the entrance of the cave.

"What are you doing here, Elijah?" God asked him again. Elijah repeated the complaint that he'd rehearsed for forty days: "I have been very zealous for the LORD God Almighty," he said. "The Israelites have rejected Your covenant, broken down Your altars, and put Your prophets to death with the sword. I am the only one left, and now they are trying to kill me, too."

"Go back," God told him. "You are not alone. I have seven thousand in Israel whose knees have not bowed down to Baal and all whose mouths have not kissed him." All spoken in a still, small voice.

For some reason, all of those who follow God—even the most godly among us—occasionally deceive ourselves into thinking that we should never encounter trouble when we are serving Him. Instead, we presume our paths should be strewn with roses and everyone we meet should immediately get with the program. Then, when we find opposition, we're shocked and we run, frightened and worried. Our peace is shattered. In the midst of terror and trouble, the clamor of tribulation is often all we hear, and the confusion ringing in our own hearts gives us faulty instruction. Our fright when Satan rattles his sabers—or our very human doubts—are not a surprise to God. When we have questions, He's prepared to answer them. When we have confusions, He's prepared to clear them up. When we have fears, He's prepared to assuage them. But like Elijah who was expecting God to carve a memo on the face of a rock or perform some other pyrotechnic, the power is not in the method of delivery. The power of peace is in the Word of God, even when delivered in a still, small voice.

Based on 1 Kings 19

'Til the Storm Passes By

In the dark of the midnight have I oft hid my face,
While the storms howl above me and there's no hiding place.
'Mid the crash of the thunder, precious Lord, hear my cry,
"Keep me safe 'til the storm passes by."

Many times Satan whispered, "There is no use to try,
"For there's no end of sorrow, there's no hope by and by."
But I know Thou art with me, and tomorrow I'll rise
Where the storms never darken the skies.

When the long night has ended, and the storms come no more,
Let me stand in Thy presence on that bright, peaceful shore.
In that land where the tempest never comes, Lord may I
Dwell with Thee when the storm passes by.

'Til the storm passes over, 'til the thunder sounds no more,
'Til the clouds roll forever from the sky,
Hold me fast, let me stand in the hollow of Thy hand;
Keep me safe 'til the storm passes by.

MOSIE LISTER

Listening for the Voice of Peace

When a terrible case of laryngitis left me almost totally without a voice, and a bad haircut made me look like a member of the House of Lords at the same time, I considered getting a bicycle horn and renaming myself Harpo Marx. Whatever was wrong in my vocal cords had so compressed my voice that any sound was a series of high-pitched peeps. It was a good thing we lived far inland or whales and dolphins could have beached themselves on my unintended command! The kids were thrilled, and my voice was funny to everyone else but embarrassing and very frustrating to me. The haircut I could live with, but I had a ton of business to transact, some of which called on my ability to state disputed facts; but I was having a hard time being effective while sounding like Smurfette.

Finally, the doctor told me to quit using my voice altogether, and I entered a strange new world devoid of my two-cents' worth on any and all subjects. Funny thing, though, except for answering the telephone and ordering fast food, it didn't make too much difference in the day-to-day of life. Instead, people I encountered did all the talking. All I needed to do was listen, smile with understanding, nod "yes" and shake "no," and no one seemed to notice the difference. I thought of lots of things I wanted to say, but no one would have heard me but dogs and bats. I wondered if that was what it was like to be God, to have everyone else do all the talking and no one but Him do any listening. I wondered how often I had rattled off a list of to-dos for God, but didn't stop to listen to what He had to say to me. I wondered how many times I had not heard His voice, only my own. I wondered how much wisdom, comfort, and peace I had forfeited because I had not listened for the still, small voice.

The Comforter, the Purveyor of Peace

But the Comforter, which is the Holy Ghost,
whom the Father will send in my name,
He shall teach you all things,
and bring all things to your remembrance,
whatsoever I have said unto you.
Peace I leave with you,
my peace I give unto you:
not as the world giveth, give I unto you.
Let not your heart be troubled,
neither let it be afraid.
JOHN 14:26–27

Jesus promised to send a
"Comforter" to the disciples,
the Holy Spirit. . . .
What does the Spirit do?
He enables us to be all that
God has saved us to be and to do.
He is not the kind of comforter
who simply pats us on the back
and encourages us
to carry out God's will.
In other words,
He gives us the backbone to live
and to proclaim the truth.

TONY EVANS

Eden is the fragrance of the fruit of the Spirit. In that idyllic garden, there was no fear because there was no sin. There were no crushing disappointments or failures. God was at one with man and woman, and they with Him. The fruit of the Spirit is Eden's peace. Peace is the state God created and sin destroyed. It's the condition Jesus restored to believers through His death on the cross.

JAMES ALDERMAN

Emergency Numbers When You Need Christ's Peace

- When you are in sorrow—call John 14.
- When men fail you—call Psalm 27.
- If you want to be fruitful—call John 15.
- When you have sinned—call Psalm 51.
- When you worry—call Matthew 6:19–34.
- When you are in danger—call Psalm 91.
- When God seems far away—call Psalm 139.
- When your faith needs stirring—call Hebrews 11.
- When you are lonely and fearful—call Psalm 23.
- When you grow bitter and critical—call 1 Corinthians 13.

- For Paul's secret to happiness—call Colossians 3:12–17.
- For understanding of Christianity—call 2 Corinthians 5:15–19.
- When you feel down and out—call Romans 8:31.
- When you want peace and rest—call Matthew 11:25–30.
- When the world seems bigger than God—call Psalm 90.
- When you want Christian assurance—call Romans 8:1–30.
- When you leave home for labor or travel—call Psalm 121.
- When your prayers grow narrow or selfish—call Psalm 67.
- For a great invention/opportunity—call Isaiah 55.
- When you want courage for a task—call Joshua 1.
- For how to get along with fellow men—call Romans 12.
- When you think of investments and returns—call Mark 10.
- If you are depressed—call Psalm 27.
- If your pocketbook is empty—call Psalm 37.
- If you are losing confidence in people—call 1 Corinthians 13.

- If people seem unkind—call John 15.
- If you are discouraged about your work—call Psalm 126.
- If you find the world growing small and yourself great—call Psalm 19.

Alternate numbers:

- For dealing with fear—call Psalm 34:7.
- For security—call Psalm 121:3.
- For assurance—call Mark 8:35.
- For reassurance—call Psalm 145:18.

Emergency numbers may be dialed direct. No operator assistance is necessary. All lines to heaven are open twenty-four hours a day!

The Author of Life and Peace

From Korea, a pastor reports that he strategically located his newly formed church next to a prison because he felt a burden for the men on death row. A few months after beginning his prison ministry, a Buddhist monk approached the pastor and asked, "What are you telling these men?"

The pastor was confused by the monk's inquiry. "I don't understand your question," he replied.

The monk responded, "I have been working here for many years, and I have watched the men walk down the hallway to die. I could hear and see fear in each inmate—until now. The men you talk to seem to be at peace. So I want to know what you tell these men that I don't."

"It is simple," the pastor told the monk. "We don't talk about death and what awaits them on the other side of the door. We talk about Jesus Christ—the Author of life."

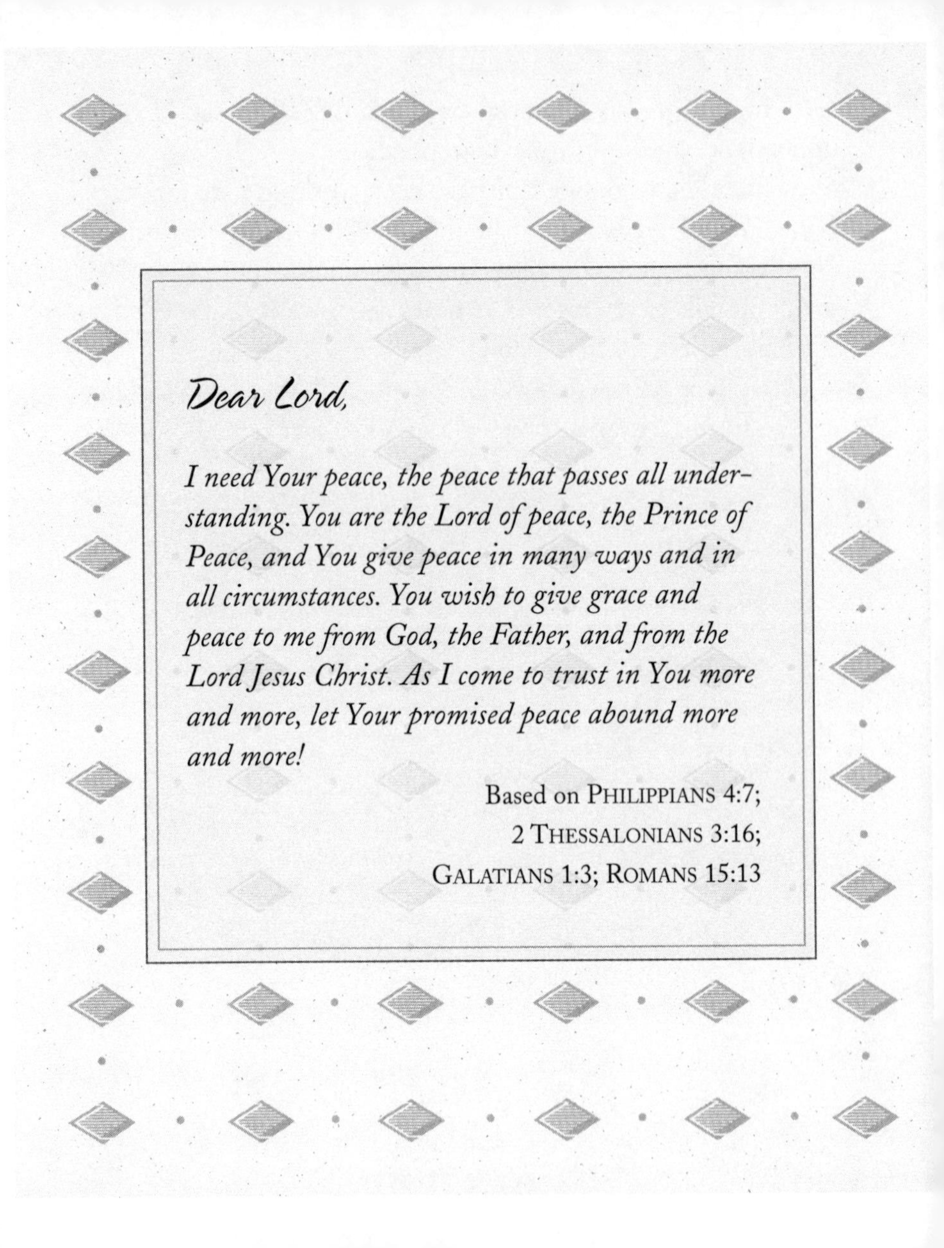

Dear Lord,

I need Your peace, the peace that passes all understanding. You are the Lord of peace, the Prince of Peace, and You give peace in many ways and in all circumstances. You wish to give grace and peace to me from God, the Father, and from the Lord Jesus Christ. As I come to trust in You more and more, let Your promised peace abound more and more!

Based on PHILIPPIANS 4:7;
2 THESSALONIANS 3:16;
GALATIANS 1:3; ROMANS 15:13

Chapter 2

Planting the Holy Seeds of Peace

So I say, live by the Spirit, and you will not gratify the desires of the sinful nature. For the sinful nature desires what is contrary to the Spirit, and the Spirit what is contrary to the sinful nature. They are in conflict with each other, so that you do not do what you want. But if you are led by the Spirit, you are not under law. The acts of the sinful nature are obvious: sexual immorality, impurity and debauchery; idolatry and witchcraft; hatred, discord, jealousy, fits of rage, selfish ambition, dissensions, factions and envy; drunkenness, orgies, and the like. I warn you, as I did before, that those who live like this will not inherit the kingdom of God. But the fruit of the Spirit is. . .peace. . . . Let us not become conceited, provoking and envying each other.

GALATIANS 5:16–22, 26 NIV

There were two of them, garish with showy armor, prickly with weapons, and arrogant in attitude. Strutting boldly, they loudly appraised the village girls and women whose misfortune it was to be on the streets at that moment. They commented leeringly on their feminine attributes, as if they were choosing a carnal conquest, which was precisely what these soldiers were doing.

Helpless, angry, and unarmed, the men of Nazareth watched in silent impotence, smoldering with hatred, as one of the soldiers boldly peered down inside the tunic front of a very young woman.

"Look here!" he called to his companion. "The gods have favored this one! Let's take her!"

Finding the fabric to be a hindrance to their ungodly pursuits, they tore open her clothing exposing her nakedness. As they exclaimed over their prize, the Nazarene villagers, seething in silent fury, modestly turned their faces away from the wailing girl and the lustful men. This was just one more outrage that they had to bear until the Messiah would deliver them.

Now as never before, every new mother in Israel born of the line of David anxiously searched the face of her newborn son, hoping against hope that her baby might be the Messiah. The nation desperately needed a Messiah, but the heavens seemed to be silent, and many in Israel were feeling abandoned by God.

The Romans had brought their heathen culture, gods, and immoral ideas to Israel. They carelessly trampled the tender vine of God's anointed people under an armored boot of imperialism. Rome was the master; Israel their unwilling slave. Equally as distressing, more and more of God's people were falling prey to the siren song of Roman materialism. Where was Jehovah God? Where was the God of Abraham, Isaac, Jacob, and Moses? If He didn't hurry, would there be any righteous left in Israel?

From her hiding place in an alley, Mary saw, with a heavy heart, the misfortunes of the young woman. Just as easily, it could have been her. As a betrothed woman, she kept her head and face covered to avert curious, bold eyes, but that didn't stop the Roman soldiers, a fact she had just witnessed. Soldiers weren't supposed to do that sort of thing but the powers-that-were just looked the other direction when they did.

As the woman's screams grew more distant and faint, Mary stepped out and quickly finished her errand. Having grown up in Nazareth, she knew the back streets, the small secret crannies and dark byways where a person could go from one part of town to the other, so she used those passages to thread her way home. They were inconvenient, but they tended to be safer.

As she slipped into a blind passageway, a tall, bright man

stepped out of the shadows, startling her. He was larger, far more muscular than the soldiers. Even without armor, he glowed like the sun.

"Greetings, you who are highly favored! The Lord is with you!"

At his words, Mary blanched in fear, her eyes flickering from side to side searching for a route of escape. *What kind of greeting might this be?* she wondered.

The bright person identified himself. "Do not be afraid," he told her. "I am Gabriel."

Instantly, Mary recognized the name from the Scriptures she had studied. Gabriel was the angel dispatched from God to the prophet Daniel when Israel was held captive by Babylon. This was the very angel that foretold Israel's deliverance! Her eyes wide with wonder, she turned her full attention to him.

"Mary, you have found favor with God," he told her, smiling broadly, the corners of his eyes crinkling with gladness in anticipation of presenting his news. "You will be with child and give birth to a son, and you are to give Him the name Jesus. He will be great and will be called the Son of the Most High. The Lord God will give Him the throne of His father David, and He will reign over the house of Jacob forever; His kingdom will never end."

A hundred questions raced through Mary's mind. She did not doubt the bright being's identity or message—although it astonished her to think that God was mindful of her in her low estate—but she abruptly remembered the violent scene in the market and she recalled her espousal to Joseph the carpenter. She had made a pledge; she had certain responsibilities.

"How will this be," Mary asked the angel, "since I am a virgin?" This was a question worth asking. Gabriel understood it, and although many people feel that it is wrong to question the will of God, neither the angel—nor the Almighty—was offended. When God asks us to cooperate, when He breaks into our lives, He does so with the finesse of the truest gentleman. Not that the Lord God Almighty, the Creator of heaven and earth couldn't demand that we conform to His will and force us to His purpose—although if He did, it would be His right and privilege—however, it wouldn't be His way. God was sending His Son to be born from Mary's womb. His advent would cause upheaval in her young life. She had made promises to Joseph. It was only right that Mary should ask how His will was to be accomplished and what she should do to facilitate it. God and His plans could easily withstand any questions.

The angel answered, "The Holy Spirit will come upon you, and the power of the Most High will overshadow you. So the Holy One to be born of you will be called the Son of God."

Mary digested this news. She didn't understand everything that Gabriel was telling her; she did know that she would experience something that was unique in the annals of biology and history. She knew the old Jewish saying, "Every birth has three partners: the mother, the father, and the Holy Spirit," yet somehow, those three elements would take on a new form. She had enough information to say an unqualified "Yes!" to the purpose of God; however, true to His practice, God offered to supply evidence that the angel was His messenger, and what he was telling her was true.

"Even Elizabeth your relative is going to have a child in her old age, and she who was said to be barren is in her sixth month. For nothing is impossible with God!" the angel told her.

Mary heard his words and marveled in joy. Israel would have a Deliverer born from her own body! And Elizabeth would have a child! How could she refuse the Almighty?

"I am the Lord's servant," Mary answered him. "May it be to me as you have said."

And so the Prince of Peace was conceived. As the days wore on and the legitimacy of her pregnancy was questioned and the child's life was threatened, these moments became more important to her peace of mind. She could point back to the moment when the angel had told her that she had found favor with God and would bear the Christ. God had answered her questions and offered evidence. It was the peace of God in the storms of life that made Mary ponder and treasure these things in her heart.

Based on LUKE 1; LUKE 2:51

Moved by the Spirit

Although Katie's parents took her to church every time the doors were open, by age eleven she still had not made a profession of faith in God. However, God had plans that changed her life.

Her church was having revival services, and although Katie felt convicted by the Holy Spirit to go to the altar and make peace with God, she strongly resisted going. "It was on the seventh and last night of services," she recalled, "and I felt like I had fooled the evangelist and outfoxed God because I had not been down to the altar all week. But when the evangelist gave the invitation, I had to hang on to the pew in front of me to keep myself in my seat!"

At the very end of the service, the evangelist paused before dismissing the congregation. He said, 'There's one more person here who needs to give his or her heart to Jesus.' I knew that was me—but I was not going to go. I remember that I looked at my hands on the pew in front of me and my knuckles had turned white from my holding on so tight.

"Then the evangelist said, 'If you are that person who needs to make peace with God, hold up your hand.' I looked down at the pew and realized that one of my hands was missing. I turned to look at my shoulder to see where my hand went, and my eyes followed my arm all the way up. I saw my hand in the air, and I thought, *What's it doing up there?* Then the evangelist said, 'You with your hand up, come forward!' And I went up and prayed for forgiveness.

"That night when I went to bed, I barely touched the sheets! I felt as if I were floating in my bed because the weight of my sins was gone. I felt clean. I had always heard the metaphor about the weight of sin, but I experienced freedom from sin that night and real peace with God. I knew I was dramatically different and I knew what I was feeling was real."

> *The result of a believing prayer is that the peace of God will stand like a sentinel on guard upon our hearts. . . . That peace of God, says Paul, passes all understanding. That does not mean that the peace of God is such a mystery that man's mind cannot understand it, although that also is true. It means that the peace of God is so precious that man's mind, with all its skill and all its knowledge, can never produce it. It can never be of man's contriving; it is only of God's giving. The way to peace is in prayer to entrust ourselves and all whom we hold dear to the loving hands of God.*
>
> WILLIAM BARCLAY

The Picture of Peace

A large painting of Christ's resurrection is skillfully rendered with careful detail. While the scene is touching, the drama behind the painting is just as poignant. The painting's creation ushered an unhappy artist from sadness and death into peace and life.

The artist, Mark, hadn't truly been happy with his life for a long time. "I had been unhappy for so long that I thought it was normal," he said. "I assumed everybody was unhappy." He suppressed his depression in his waking hours, but at night it erupted in fearful dreams of insecurity and paranoid nightmares of exposure to danger.

Meanwhile, Mark entered an art contest sponsored by the *Miami Herald* and won first prize. This success brought him some fame and a few painting commissions. Among those was a request made by his grandfather. "Grandpa came to me with this idea of doing a painting of the resurrection of Christ," Mark remembered. "I knew Grandpa had been praying for me, and actually, I think he was just trying to get me to look at the Bible. I thought, *This is somebody I respect. I'll make an effort.*

He borrowed a Bible to check out the details of the resurrection. Now, with the eyes of an artist and adult, he saw anew the story he had heard so often as a child. Using his refreshed understanding of the story, he found models to pose, took photographs, and began work. "It was frustrating, but I just couldn't make much progress on the painting," said Mark. "Although I was far away from God, I realized I needed God's help—so I got down on my knees and asked. My only interest, though, was just to finish this painting."

But a week or so later, Mark had a dream that made him realize he needed God. "In my dream I was making this amorphous sculpture, and I suddenly had a revelation that I was being influenced by the devil," said Mark. "He had been influencing me and causing me problems. Then I saw this nondescript mummy-like creature run away. The devil had been influencing me and my mind, and when I unmasked him, he ran away." The short, odd dream gave him pause. "I thought, *If the devil is real, I want to get in touch with God and get on His side!*"

Some time later, Mark met some people who invited him to a Bible study. Although he had been a passive hearer of the gospel as a child, he had never before sat down and studied the Bible for the purpose of understanding it and learning about God for himself. Now, his study of the Bible, along with his association with believers, made his life suddenly more enjoyable.

Mark eventually became involved in campus ministry, dedicated his life to the Lord, and was baptized. This time, when Mark began again to work on the resurrection painting, it didn't take him very long, not more than a week or two. "I had a different outlook on life," said Mark. "Now I was on God's side and at peace with Him; I realized God had been on my side all along. Living in the light rather than living in the darkness gave me a sense of direction and reason to be hopeful. At last I had true peace of mind."

> *As a man lives in the air, the man whose life is dominated by the Spirit of God lives in Christ and is never separated from Him. As he breathes in the air and the air fills him, so Christ fills him. He has no mind of his own; Christ is his mind. He has no desires of his own; the will of Christ is his only law. He is Spirit-controlled, Christ-controlled, God-focused.*
>
> WILLIAM BARCLAY

Perennial Peace

Perennials are great plants! They grow year after year, surviving drought, freezing temperatures, and transplanting. With a little proper care, they multiply and get hardier, healthier, and increasingly lovely.

Peace from the Holy Spirit has many of the same qualities.

No matter how difficult life becomes, God's peace is available to you time and time again—if you take time to plant and cultivate it. Here's how:

- *Prepare your heart to receive peace.* God wants to implant His Holy Spirit in you and bring you peace. Be open to what the Holy Spirit wants to do in your life. Ask Him to indwell you and pull up the weeds and thorns—the cares of this world. Clear out the rocks—the uncaring, selfish attitudes. Break up the hard places—the areas where you lack faith. And shoo away the birds—in other words, guard your mind from Satan's influence (Luke 8:4–8). Then you will become fertile ground for much fruit. The Master Gardener can do beautiful things with your life.

- *Plant God's Word in your heart by study and meditation.* If you don't plant the Word of God within you, it won't just suddenly appear. However, if you take the time and effort to make the Word a part of your mind and heart, even when the harsh, wintry winds of adversity blow, you will find strength.

Seeds Well Planted

Carl's life has now spanned nearly ninety years, and during most of that time, his body has done pretty much whatever he commanded it to do. A few years ago, however, his knee joints conspired together to stage a mutiny. Now, although he still has the will and the desire to go places and do things, chronic pain makes it difficult. His self-sufficient nature is frustrated.

Ever since he was a young man, however, Carl has made the study and memorization of the Scriptures a priority in his life. Although he was a poor student in school, a slow reader, and had problems memorizing, he daily spent time in the Bible. Now, in the late autumn of his years, the seeds of the gospel crop up in unexpected places—but always just at the right time.

Recently, after a particularly painful night, Carl woke up depressed about his deteriorating physical condition. Still in bed, he felt the Spirit prompt him to remember a verse he had memorized long ago. "Romans 8:31 and 32 just popped into my head," he recalled. " '. . .If God be for us, who can be against us? He that spared not his own Son, but delivered him up for us all, how shall he not with him also freely give us all things?' As soon as I recited the words to myself, I had peace.

"Now, whenever I have negative thoughts, I remember these verses, and they give me comfort, assurance, and peace."

I will both
lay me down in peace,
and sleep:
for thou, LORD,
only makest me dwell in safety.

PSALM 4:8

The Shelter for the Battered Soul

Peace begins with God. He is the fountain and source of all peace. Every shred of peace which we discover is two things at the same moment: It is a gift of God and a discovery of the human heart. But it must always be remembered that we never create peace; we receive peace from God. We must also remember that peace from God comes in four ways: Peace comes from earnest seeking. God gave us minds, and it is often through our minds that God speaks peace to our souls. With our minds, we learn the truth about God in the sunny seasons. In stormy times of uncertainty, that truth is applied like a sweet healing balm to our wounds and a shelter to our battered souls. The peace of God will be a stunted fruit in the lives of people who are too lazy to cultivate knowledge of Him within their minds.

Peace comes by connection to the Holy Spirit. The Holy Spirit is the Teacher, Counselor, and the Illuminator of the mysteries of life. As the apostle Paul wrote, the Scriptures and the workings of God are a mystery to those who are without the Holy Spirit. He brings to mind what we have learned of God and applies those truths to our situation.

Peace comes by reverent waiting. Here is an interesting dichotomy: We actively seek God's peace while we patiently, respectfully wait for it. We need to strenuously seek His truth while waiting quietly in prayer and study. However, prayer and study are not passive activities. They are intense, dedicated, concentrated listening for the voice of God. Peace comes as a gift. Peace is yours as a child of God. Because your faithful Father said so, believe it and claim it. Count on it. Ask for it. Thank Him in advance of receiving it.

A Shelter in the Time of Storm

The Lord's our rock, in Him we hide,
A shelter in the time of storm;
Secure whatever ill betide,
A shelter in the time of storm.

O Jesus is a rock in a weary land,
A weary land; a weary land;
O Jesus is a rock in a weary land,
A shelter in the time of storm.

VERNON J. CHARLESWORTH

Thou wilt keep him in perfect peace, whose mind is stayed on thee: because he trusteth in thee. ISAIAH 26:3

A Steadfast Mind

Keeping your mind "steadfast" upon God is a good way to live. As His thoughts and ways fill your mind, you will reap peace, prosperity, divine help and guidance, and much, much more. Here are some suggestions for keeping Him utmost in your mind:

- *Learn spiritual and scriptural songs.* The words and messages will stick with you, and you will find yourself humming or whistling them as you work or play. (One particularly difficult day at my high-pressure office, I began whistling "Jesus Loves Me" in the halls as I moved from place to place. I was pleasantly pleased—and a little amused—to find even the most vicious, cutthroat executives humming "Jesus Loves Me" as they went from meeting to meeting. By lunchtime, the entire mood in the place had lightened.)

- *Learn Scripture.* If this is a new exercise for you, start with one verse a week copied on a sticky note or three-by-five-inch card and stuck in a place where you do some mindless task. While you are completing that task, work on memorizing the verse.

- *Set aside a time just for Jesus.* Try not to double up your quiet time with the Lord with other activities. He deserves quality time. Use the quiet time alone with Him to read your Bible, praise Him, worship Him, and pray.

- *Water well with prayer.* While the prairies where I live are fertile, they tend to be dry. Farmers often plow and plant, have their crops sprout up lush and green—and then have the heavens turn to brass and produce no rain. In times of drought like these, it really makes no difference whether or not the ground is cleared, planted, and fertilized; it simply won't produce. Our relationship with God is much the same. If we don't talk or listen to Him, we won't have any fruit in our relationship. We don't need to use long words or poetic phrases in our prayers; we can simply speak to Him as favored children to a loving father, because that is the relationship He wishes to have with us.

Find some fellow believers from the family of God with which to share your faith. I come from a big family with five brothers and two sisters. We are close and love one another dearly even though we are separated by many miles. Because I live so far away, I can't always share in all of the family celebrations. However, although I have lived in this area only a very short time, I have found a beautiful family of Christian believers here. They include us in their holiday celebrations. If I have a need, all I have to do is mention it to my sisters in Christ and I know they will throw their arms around me and pray for me on the spot. If they have a sorrow, they know they can call me. If I were to stray from the Lord, I have no doubt one of them would lovingly correct me. I learned a lot about Christ from my biological family, but I've also learned a great deal from the family of God. They help keep my mind on Him.

Evening Prayer

O Lord my God, I thank Thee that Thou hast brought this day to a close:

I thank Thee that Thou hast given me peace in body and
in soul.

Thy hand has been over me and has protected and
preserved me.

Forgive my puny faith, the ill that I this day have done,
And help me to forgive all who have wronged me.

Grant me a quiet night's sleep beneath Thy tender care,
And defend me from all the temptations of darkness.

Into Thy hands I commend my loved ones,
And all who dwell in this house;
I commend my body and soul.

DIETRICH BONHOEFFER

Let us then approach the throne of grace with confidence, so that we may receive mercy and find grace to help us in our time of need.

HEBREWS 4:16 NIV

Rejoice in the Lord always. I will say it again: Rejoice! Let your gentleness be evident to all. The Lord is near. Do not be anxious about anything, but in everything, by prayer and petition, with thanksgiving, present your requests to God. And the peace of God, which transcends all understanding, will guard your hearts and your minds in Christ Jesus.

PHILIPPIANS 4:4–7 NIV

"Don't worry, Pray!" Paul says. And notice the immediate result—peace. Even before our prayers are answered, there is peace. Before we have any idea how things will work out, there is peace. Why? Because by our crying out to God and unloading our cares and burdens on Him, He is assured of (and we are reminded of) our dependence on Him. And that is His priority; that is what pleases Him.

CHARLES STANLEY

Paul said we should make our requests to God with thanksgiving. Then we should thank Him for answering when we ask, and quit worrying about the problem or situation. This is the prayer of faith. If we don't think God is going to do something, why ask? If we're going to continue to worry, that is not trust. And without trust, we will never experience a rich harvest of peace.

Dear Lord,

I realize that if I continue to sow my life according to my flesh, I'll reap a harvest of bitterness, unrest, and destruction. But as I sow according to the Spirit, I will reap peace. I acknowledge Jesus as the Source of all peace. He broke down the walls of sin that separated me from God that He might reconcile me both to God and to those around me. He has created this peace through His blood shed on the cross. I accept Him and His sacrifice; I accept Jesus as my Lord and Prince of Peace.

Based on EPHESIANS 2:14–16

Chapter 3

Ten Perennial Questions about Peace— Or the Lack of It

Fear thou not; for I am with thee: be not dismayed; for I am thy God: I will strengthen thee; yea, I will help thee; yea, I will uphold thee with the right hand of my righteousness.

ISAIAH 41:10

1. *I've done some wrong things in my life. Can I have peace with God?*

Yes, you can—by admitting you're a sinner and asking forgiveness. You say, "I have done some things wrong, but I am basically a good person!" Well, you may do some good things, but the Bible says, "There is none righteous, no, not one" (Romans 3:10). And no excuses work here. To become right with God, we all have to admit that we are sinners, regardless of what good we have done and what excuses we may have.

As a sinner, you are separated from God—and that, in a nutshell, is why you do not have peace. The discomfort you feel—the lack of peace—is the Holy Spirit turning the searchlight of holiness upon your soul. He doesn't do this to embarrass you, but to point out your need for Him. Admitting sinfulness is a very tall hurdle for many people to clear; but once we do, our souls find refreshment in simply being honest with God. And believe me; God will not be shocked by our admissions of sinfulness. He already knows.

Once you confess your sinfulness, you need to ask forgiveness. Say a simple prayer like this: "God, I am a sinner. Please forgive me." There is no need for fancy prayers. God already knows you better than you know yourself. He won't be one whit impressed if you opt for big words. It is you whom He loves—the real you whom you think no one knows about—and He longs for you to communicate with Him honestly. He longs for a loving relationship with you—His child.

2. *I've done some really bad things in my life. Can God really forgive me?*

Are you a murderer? Moses was a murderer—he murdered an Egyptian with his bare hands and had to hide. Once he patched things up with God, he not only became God's instrument of deliverance for His people, but also authored the first five books of the Bible. God delivered His Law to Moses's blood-stained but forgiven hands, and on one occasion, spoke to him face-to-face. The apostle Paul falls into the same category as Moses, only he was responsible for the deaths and torture of many more people, including women and children. God chose Paul to spread His Word. Paul also authored a good share of the New Testament.

Are you a felon? The first person Jesus brought to heaven was a felon—the thief on the cross. Are you an adulterer? Jesus said to the woman caught in the very act of adultery, "Neither do I condemn you. Go now and leave your life of sin." He is saying the same to you. His forgiveness is available, regardless of the sins you have committed. Ask His forgiveness—and leave your sins behind.

3. *I may have committed the unforgivable sin. Is there hope for me?*

What might your unforgivable sin be? Mass murder? God forgave the apostle Paul of that. Sexual sin? He forgave King

David of that. Stealing? He forgave the thief on the cross. So long as your heart is turning toward God, He is eager to forgive you, no matter what you may have done. The only time He can't forgive you is when you turn away from Him.

4. *I believe in God, but I'm not so sure about Jesus. Is it really necessary to ask Jesus to be my Lord and Savior to have peace?*

Yes. Jesus Christ is the only way to true peace.

> *Enter through the narrow gate. For wide is the gate and broad is the road that leads to destruction, and many enter through it. But small is the gate and narrow the road that leads to life, and only a few find it.*
>
> MATTHEW 7:13–14 NIV

Jesus is the only path that leads to heaven and peace.

> *I am the way and the truth and the life. No one comes to the Father except through me.* JOHN 14:6 NIV

Jesus knew most people would reject Him because most people prefer to fashion their own ideas of God. They worship the god of their imagination so that they will not have to die to self and learn how to truly love. If you don't like or appreciate Jesus and His message of selfless love, you won't care for God too much either—because if you know Jesus, you know God.

He that hath seen me
hath seen the Father.

JOHN 14:9

5. *I have done things in my past that I am ashamed of. God may forgive me—but how do I make peace with those things?*

Many people are haunted by their past. Some fear the past will come back to expose them for what they truly are—sinners. Some have genuine, heartrending anguish over the price they and others have had to pay for their misdeeds. And truth be told, most all of us are struggling with the fallout from stupid, wrong decisions that we made somewhere, sometime in our past. The past cannot be changed, but it must be dealt with honestly, with the help and grace of God.

Jesus is the great Salvager of lives. The angels announced to the shepherds, "He is the Savior, Christ the Lord." Don't expect Him to magically transform the difficult mate you chose to marry—but count on Him to be your Comforter and the Lover of your soul. Don't expect Him to erase illegitimate children from your life—but count on Him to be the Father to the fatherless. Don't expect Him to give you a new set of parents—but ask Him to make your parents new. Don't expect Him to give you a totally new set of circumstances—but you can count on Him to make you a totally new person and salvage your life. Believe Him when He promises, "I will restore to you the years that the locust hath eaten" (Joel 2:25). God can restore the lost years by giving you joy in the present one.

If Christ has forgiven you and taken your sins upon Himself, you need to let Him have them. His sacrifice for your sin is sufficient. If you continue to whip yourself for your sin, in essence you are saying the punishment Christ took for your sin was not enough. Remember: It is by His stripes we are healed (Isaiah 53:5)—not by the beatings you inflict upon yourself. Doing this will bring you nothing but mental and emotional pain. Wearing a hair shirt knit from your past transgressions will only make you chafed—not forgiven.

Why walk around with a memory splinter stuck in your mind? Would you leave a wood or steel splinter stuck in your eye or hand? . . . Splinters can fester. . . . What can be done? I know a very ancient remedy. His name is Jesus, and He can heal bad memories.

DR. ROBERT S. MASERONI

6. *God may forgive me, but others continue to remind me of my mistakes. How can I have peace?*

Consider reminders of your past mistakes as opportunities to testify to the forgiving power and grace of Jesus Christ. You might answer the charges of others like this: "Yes, I did what you say. I sinned, and I am forgiven by the grace and power of Jesus' sacrifice." As one woman said after she confessed her sin of adultery to God and her husband, "I'm free! You may not forgive me, but Jesus has! He doesn't condemn me even if you do!"

Of course, we all need to make things right between ourselves and those against whom we have sinned, but we can do this from the position of a changed life now filled with the power of the Almighty God. As we admit our flaws and past mistakes, God will provide guidance and healing.

Satan wants to make us feel condemned. After all, one of his names is "accuser of the brethren." People who remind you or question you about your past may be doing Satan's work—or they may simply be looking for the same peace you now have.

> *We have to deal with the effects of sin in our lives. Once we have undergone and completed His discipline, He rejoices and welcomes us with celebration. But the road back is a hard road. We have left a trail of casualties: hurt people, broken relationships, poor choices, financial problems, and*

lots of pain—emotional and spiritual pain.

God wants us to make a comeback. He wants us to make a comeback more than we do. . . . He wants us to succeed. This is transparent, because were it not for His grace, none of us would ever be able to make a comeback. He finds us; we don't find Him.

PATRICK M. MORLEY

7. *How do I make peace with someone who hates me or has hurt me?*

Sometimes you can't. God Himself longs for everyone to be at peace, but that hasn't happened yet. However, you can do two things:

Pray for the person. Prayer is our secret weapon; Jesus Himself told us to pray for our enemies. When people hurt you, pray that God will open their eyes to the love of Jesus. Ask the Holy Spirit to convict them of their sin. They won't know what—or Who—hit them!

At the same time, ask God to give you His unconditional love for your enemy.

A woman whose church deacon father molested her for much of her childhood wrote: "The scars that my father inflicted upon me seemed so deep as to be uneraseable. My tendency was and still is to mistrust everyone, including God.

After all, God knew what was happening. Why didn't He stop my father? But as long as I held to that way of thinking, there was no healing for me. I learned that I needed to handle my victimization the same way Jesus handled His. I needed to offer forgiveness to my enemy, even though he wouldn't acknowledge his sin against me. I needed to love him with God's love —regardless.

"As soon as I asked God to help me love my father in spite of everything he did to me, I began to have peace with my past. My father has never admitted what he did to me and has never asked for my forgiveness. He may never face up to his crime. But I no longer hate him. I pity him, but I don't hate him. My father's sins are between him and God. I can't change him; I can only change myself."

Be kind to those who hate you. They won't be able to figure out what you are up to! We are told to love our enemies so the next time someone is nasty to you, send him or her flowers. The Bible calls it "heaping coals of fire upon their heads" —which simply means, they'll be embarrassed and ashamed. Trust God to take care of you and don't worry about those who hate you. Believe me, He knows how to take care of His own beloved children!

8. *How do I make peace with someone I have hurt?*

Humbly go to the person, admit your mistake, and ask for forgiveness. What happens after that is that person's responsibility. If you can restore what you have damaged, you should do so.

9. *I feel so guilty all the time, even when I have repented. Why don't I have peace?*

The enemy is deceiving you. This is an old ruse Satan uses to destroy a Christian's peace. In spite of being such a frequently used, threadbare trick, Satan keeps on using it because it works so well—especially with new believers.

Note Matt's experience:

> "While I was in college, a new Christian, and deeply involved in a campus Bible study group, I became acutely aware of the sin in my life," said Matt. "I was just learning what sin was and how I sinned every day. Realizing how weak I was and how often I gave in to sin made me discouraged. One moment I'd be asking God's forgiveness, and the next I'd be sinning again. I'd get depressed and feel bad about it."

A group of preachers on campus regularly spoke on the quad area where the students could hear them while coming and going to classes. One particular day, as Matt walked across campus, he heard a message that brought him peace. "The preacher was making the point that God loves us and wants to help us," said Matt. "That Jesus didn't come to condemn the world, but through His sacrifice, He came to save us. I thought, *Yeah! That's right! I'm a sinner, but God didn't send Jesus to punish me but to love me!* All my discouragement just melted away and I had peace after that. I don't suppose that preacher ever knew how much he helped me."

Jesus told Nicodemus, a religious teacher obsessed with keeping the Law of Moses, "For God did not send his Son into the world to condemn the world, but to save the world through him" (John 3:17 NIV). Memorize that verse, and when the accuser comes to torment you with your past, clout him with John 3:17.

10. *I am fearful of the future. I know it is wrong to worry, but I just can't help myself. The end of the world seems so near. What do I do to have peace?*

Young people in the early church had that problem, too. In fact, because they were so persecuted and the future on earth was so bleak while the glories of heaven were so bright, many took their own lives. They had failed to grasp the true peace that Jesus offers.

I, too, believe that Christ's return is imminent. However, to be fair, I have to admit that my grandmother, born in the 1880s, also believed Christ would return in her lifetime. The disciples thought Christ would return in their lifetime—more than 2000 years ago. We're all still waiting.

Jesus will return—but we do not know the hour or the day (Mark 13:32). However, if you have an urgency about His return, you need to allow it to prompt you into action to reach the lost rather than to make you nervous with anxiety. God will give you what you need during any time of testing that may lie ahead—even if it's not the end of the whole world, just the end of your world. He will supply your needs. Like any good father, God gives His children what they need when they need it. If sometime in your future you need courage, He will supply it. If you need wisdom, He will give it.

> *Seek first his kingdom and his righteousness, and all these things will be given to you as well. Therefore do not worry about tomorrow, for tomorrow will worry about itself. Each day has enough trouble of its own.*
>
> MATTHEW 6:33–34 NIV

Lack of peace affects every portion of a person. It keeps the mind uneasy, frustrated, tormented, and incapable of concentration; it makes the soul restless, and it creates actual physical illnesses. But once you place yourself by faith into the healing arms of Jesus, the wounds left by anxiety and fear are so completely healed you may even forget how you came by the scars! Jesus wants you to be at peace.

Peace for Revenge

Jonah previously thought of hell in terms of fire. However, each time the leviathan opened its mouth to swallow gallons of plankton, he got a much wetter picture of the judgment of God. The big fish fed regularly, about every fifteen minutes or so, and Jonah dreaded each salty dose of seawater that filled its belly and threatened to drown him.

Ruefully, he remembered that the last time he had truly slept was during a violent storm aboard the ship that was supposed to take him to Tarshish, away from Nineveh, and away from the eyes of God. Now, he hoped that God would see him in the belly of the great fish and take pity upon him. Not that he deserved pity—or forgiveness—but he was hoping.

Previous to taking up residency inside the fish, Jonah had held strong opinions about whom God should forgive and for whom the fires of hell should be stoked to the maximum eternal inferno. In his estimation, if ever a people deserved damnation, the Assyrian city of Nineveh was a top candidate. Those people had long made life a misery for Israel.

What's more, God knew it, too, and He had had enough of them. He had notified Jonah to go to Nineveh and warn them concerning their great wickedness in His sight. Judgment was upon them.

Good! Jonah had thought. *About time!* There was nothing he would relish more than seeing a well-deserved load of fire and brimstone rain down upon Nineveh! The day Nineveh was destroyed would spark spontaneous celebrations in the streets of Israel! But there was a niggling element of risk to delivering God's message: If Jonah preached about the wrath of God coming upon them—a delicious thought!—there was the off-chance that the city might repent.

Even the thought of Nineveh, sitting in luxury on the rich banks of the Tigris River, fat and satiated on the blood, sweat, and flesh of Jewish slaves thoroughly sickened Jonah. Even with their long history of atrocities against the people of God, if Nineveh were to repent, God would forgive them and spare them. That thought was even more revolting to him.

Repentance cannot happen! thought Jonah. *It must not*

happen! Let them perish!

After sleepless nights wrestling with the Spirit of God, Jonah had made his decision: He headed for the Mediterranean Sea coast and bought a boat ticket for Tarshish, out of the boundaries of Israel and as far from Nineveh as he could reasonably go. Perhaps God wouldn't find him there. While he slept in the hold, a violent storm seized the ship and threatened to drown all on board. After determining that Jonah was the culprit at the heart of the storm, the other men had thrown him overboard. As providence would have it, a specially prepared fish had swallowed him. Now here he sat in the belly of the big fish, watching squid digest, slowly being digested himself, and there wasn't much he could do about it.

He'd lost track of the days and hours—but not God's point. He had wanted to be out of God's sight; therefore, he'd been banished for his rebellion. Now he was indeed lost, engulfed in dark, deep waters at the roots of the mountains with seaweed wrapped around his head. God could leave him there, and that would be just punishment, or God could rescue him, and that would be grace, the same grace He wished to bestow on the citizens of Nineveh.

With a new rush of seawater threatening his life every quarter hour, Jonah's options were limited. This situation would not continue indefinitely. God's patience with Jonah—and the people of Nineveh—was at an end. Jonah could continue to refuse

God and die, or he could cry to Him to rescue him and promise to go to Nineveh. Then it would be the people of Nineveh's turn to cry to God or perish.

Anger, hatred, unforgiveness, the need for revenge, none of these bring peace as Jonah discovered. They only drive us farther from God and into stormy waters. They become all-consuming passions, and if we are not careful, can swallow us whole.

If we want a relationship with God and want to experience His peace, we have to relinquish those things to God, no matter how justified we feel in clinging to them. Somewhere, like Jonah, we have to cry to God for release and agree to be obedient to Him. It may mean returning a gentle word for an angry one. It may mean doing a kindness to your enemy. It may mean going to Nineveh—or a family reunion.

When Jonah came to that realization—and it took three days, three nights, and repeated soakings—God spoke to the fish, and it vomited Jonah on dry land. He quickly headed for Nineveh.

When we come to the same realization, our conflicts will release us to do God's bidding and experience His peace.

Based on JONAH 1 and 2

Peace—It Is Well with My Soul

If any man deserved a vacation, it was Chicago attorney and businessman Horatio Spafford. The Chicago fire had destroyed a good deal of his real estate holdings, but instead of focusing on rebuilding his own fortune, Spafford, a devoted Christian, and his wife, Anna, threw themselves into helping the many who had lost everything in the blaze. Shortly thereafter, they buried a young son.

So in the autumn of 1873, Spafford and Anna booked passage aboard the *Ville de Havre,* a large French steamer heading for Europe. They would have a holiday with their four little girls, Maggie, Tanetta, Annie, and Bessie (ranging in age from twelve years to eighteen months).

Every honest, caring man must admit to a little apprehension when his wife and children must go somewhere without his protection. Spafford, too, must have felt some trepidation, for when business concerns made him cancel his plans to accompany them, he switched their cabin reservations from the front of the vessel to midship. He saw them off, promising to join them shortly.

The first part of the voyage was uneventful, but halfway across, off the coast of Newfoundland, their steamer collided with an English sailing vessel. The damage was massive and catastrophic; the gaping hole in the hull took in water so rapidly that the ship sank in twenty minutes. As the icy waters of the North Atlantic lapped at their feet, Anna Spafford held her four little girls and prayed with them. Then, one at a time, the waves pulled the children from their mother's arms. Unconscious and near death, Anna was pulled from the water by a passing lifeboat.

It was ten more days until Anna and the rest of the survivors landed at Cardiff, Wales. On the other side of the sea, Spafford had been anxiously awaiting the survivors' list. Anna wired him a brief, but poignant message: "Saved—alone."

Boarding the next available ship, Spafford sailed to his wife's side. En route, the captain of the ship upon which he was sailing called him to the bridge. Pointing to the navigational chart, the captain told him that they were just passing over the spot where his four young daughters were lost at sea.

As he watched the cold gray waves heaving over the graves of his beloved children, he was gifted with a supernatural peace from the heart of a loving heavenly Father. Spafford knew he would see his children again in heaven. Then the verse from Isaiah 66:12 came to his mind: For thus saith the LORD, Behold, I will extend peace to her like a river. . . .

Sometime later, remembering the pain of the moment and the wonderful peace of God in the midst of a sea of pain, Spafford penned the following words that have become one of Christendom's most enduring hymns:

When peace, like a river, attendeth my way,
When sorrow like sea billows roll,
Whatever my lot, Thou hast taught me to say,
It is well, it is well with my soul.

My sin—O the bliss of this glorious thought—
My sin not in part, but the whole.
Is nailed to the cross, and I bear it no more:
Praise the Lord, praise the Lord, O my soul!

And, Lord, haste the day when my faith shall be sight,
The clouds be rolled back as a scroll:
The trump shall resound and the Lord shall descend,
"Even so"—it is well with my soul.

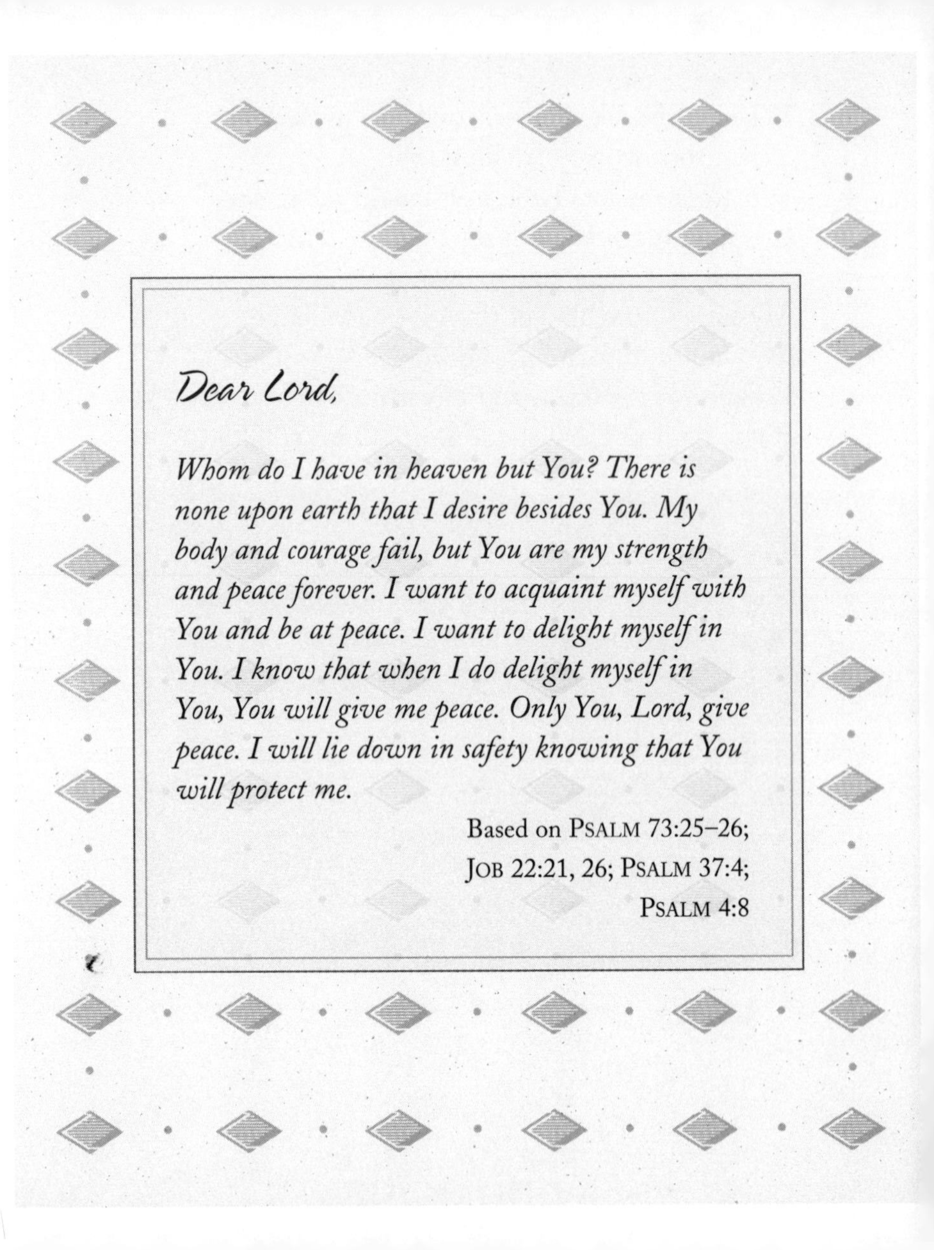

Dear Lord,

Whom do I have in heaven but You? There is none upon earth that I desire besides You. My body and courage fail, but You are my strength and peace forever. I want to acquaint myself with You and be at peace. I want to delight myself in You. I know that when I do delight myself in You, You will give me peace. Only You, Lord, give peace. I will lie down in safety knowing that You will protect me.

Based on PSALM 73:25–26;
JOB 22:21, 26; PSALM 37:4;
PSALM 4:8

Chapter 4

Peace under Attack

Those who live according to the sinful nature have their minds set on what that nature desires; but those who live in accordance with the Spirit have their minds set on what the Spirit desires. The mind of sinful man is death, but the mind controlled by the Spirit is life and peace.

Romans 8:5–6 NIV

The Path through the Thorns

Glenna was discouraged. As the adult sponsor of the church youth group, she was concerned about the influence of violent and sexually oriented music. However, when she introduced the teens to contemporary Christian music, she met with stiff resistance from an unexpected source: the youths' parents. "Some of the parents thought contemporary Christian music was of the devil because they weren't all hymns," said Glenna. "They thought the songs had the wrong beat and that the musicians just couldn't really be praising God. They said they would rather their kids listen to whatever came over the radio."

Frustrated and concerned, Glenna prayed as she drove her car across the Illinois countryside on a business trip. On her car radio, a conservative Christian radio station, one supported by her church, played soft background music. "Lord, I am confused," she prayed. "Why are these parents fighting me? Am I doing the right thing by these kids? Why am I getting all this trouble from the parents?" Just then, an interview came on the radio. It was with a Christian music group that even Glenna considered hard rock. The musicians shared a strong testimony of faith in Christ, then sang a song titled, "The Road to Zion Is in Your Heart."

"It was one of those thrilling, special moments between

me and God," Glenna recalled. "It was like He said, 'You're on the right road. You're leading them the right way. Your motives are right.' I felt such a sense of peace." Glenna said that now, many years later, she has seen the proof of that assurance she received from God. "Christian music has made a noticeable difference in the lives of many of the youth group," she said. "The message permeated their lives and helped them hold firm to their faith. I am so grateful that God guided me with His peace."

The Holy Spirit uses several spiritual markers to indicate and confirm His will. The first one is the marker of peace.

CHARLES STANLEY

Restoration After the Storm

Bonnie did not know she and her husband Paul had a problem until she opened their quarterly savings account statement.

"There was no money at all in the account," said Bonnie. "I had no idea what had happened to it. But I knew I didn't spend it."

She confronted Paul who denied that he had withdrawn any money. Bonnie knew he was lying, but she couldn't imagine what he was spending the money on until a friend told her she had seen Paul playing a video poker machine at a local filling station.

This time when Bonnie confronted Paul, he admitted he had spent their savings, but he denied he had a problem with gambling. "I can stop playing the games any time I want to," Paul told Bonnie. However, he didn't want to quit—and they soon had no money left in their checking account, either. "The games were only a quarter to play and so he'd play a game or two or three. Then an hour later, he'd come to himself and realize he'd spent a whole bunch of money," said Bonnie. "By the time I realized what he was doing, all our money was gone."

A freak winter ice storm knocked out their electricity and brought the situation to a head. "We had a gas fireplace, and Paul went downtown to get gas for it so we could have some heat. He didn't come back. Four hours later, the kids were frozen clear through, and I got in the car to go look for him," said Bonnie. She found his car at the local filling station; there, playing the video poker machine, was Paul.

"What are you doing?" Bonnie cried. "You have a wife and children who are at home freezing—and you're here wasting our money and neglecting your responsibilities!" Bonnie stormed out and went home. "I was so angry I didn't know what to do. I went into Paul's closet and took out all his clothes—and then I threw them out the front door!"

A few minutes later, Paul came home. Bonnie watched from the window as he sheepishly picked up his clothing from the front yard. "That was the breaking point," said Bonnie. "I told him I loved him, and I would help him overcome this—but he had to agree to get help."

Bonnie spent hours praying about Paul and their financial situation. She knew she needed to get her husband away from the temptation to gamble, but since all of their support system was in their home state of North Carolina, she didn't know how she was going to do it.

The answer came via a visit from one of Paul's brothers, who invited him to come north and work in the family's business there. Although this meant that Bonnie would have to leave behind her parents, extended family, friends, job, and church, she had an instantaneous peace about the move. "As soon as my brother-in-law suggested it, I just knew it was the right thing," said Bonnie. "I knew I was going to miss a lot of people, but I had a peace from God that said, 'This is the right path. Take it.' "

Peace While Scouting the Right Road

IF GOD WOULD ONLY. . .

"If God would only give me a road map," someone complained.

"No, I won't give you a road map," said God. "I'll give you The Way."

"If God would only send an angel to tell me what to do," someone complained.

"No, I won't send an angel to tell you what to do," said God. "I sent My Son to show you how to live."

"If God would only show me the truth of life, I'd live by it," someone complained.

"No, I won't just show you the truth of life," said God. "I'll give you the Truth and the Life."

"If God would only make my life perfect," someone complained.

"No, I won't make your life perfect," said God. "I'll give you Jesus to perfect you."

"If God would only send me a note to tell me His will for my life," someone complained.

"No, I won't send you a note to explain My will," said God. "I've sent you a whole Book and then I made the Word flesh to explain it to you."

"If God would only help me with my life," someone complained.

"No, I won't help you with your life," said God. "I am Life and I will live through you."

"If God had only made me wise," someone complained.

"No, I didn't make you wise," said God. "But I am Wisdom."

"If God would only bring peace on earth," someone complained.

"No, there is not peace on earth yet," said God, "but there is eternal peace for those who serve the Prince of Peace."

When we dart off in the wrong direction, we feel the hot breath of the enemy on our collars. For it is in the dark crannies that Ol' Beelzebub carries out his revolt. But there is One who sees our game-playing exhaustion and longs for us to know His rest. He understands our desire for a hiding place. He woos us to His soothing side—even when it's Him we've foolishly been hiding from—so that we might find the refuge we so desperately need.

PATSY CLAIRMONT

Christianity Is Not for Cowards

Taking a stand for Jesus, aligning yourself with His name and His cause, is similar to joining the troops inside a besieged fortress—because, my friend, we are at war. Our enemy: Satan. The battlefield: your life and mine. The prize: the eternal souls of men and women.

So here's the question: Can we have peace in the midst of a war? Or is the peace that has been promised to us through the Spirit of God something we will only experience when we lay down our lives, either on the battlefield of life or at the sound of the last trumpet of the war?

On the eve of sending His disciples into the great, eternal struggle, the Prince of Peace answered that question: "Peace I leave with you; my peace I give you. I do not give to you as the world gives. Do not let your hearts be troubled and do not be afraid" (John 14:27 NIV). Then Jesus instructed the disciples to stay attached to Himself—the Vine, to let His life flow through them via the Holy Spirit so that they would experience not only peace but an entire cornucopia of amazing spiritual fruit that buds, blossoms, and bears under the harshest conditions.

The Secret of Real Peace

Jesus gave us the secret of peace: His peace is not the peace of this world. It is a distinctly different genus. The world thinks of peace in terms of church bells ringing on a clear morning, treaties signed, bright sunrises over fertile farmland, sleeping children in flannel pajamas. . . . But the peace promised by Jesus is manifested in the midst of raging storms, in prison awaiting death by torture, when standing at the bedside of a feverish baby, when heavy boots sound outside your door, when the bank balance is nil and the bills are piled high. Pretty sunrises are no good then. We need much more!

Times like these are when the soul needs the Man who walked on water, the One who said to the waves, "Peace! Be still!"—and they quietly settled down and calmed. In times like these, peace is victorious in the war for the soul. Why? Because the Prince of Peace is reigning there.

The peace of God, the peace that is the fruit of the Spirit, is not dependent upon circumstances. It is dependent upon the love, grace, and power of God, and our obedient submission to Him. Just like God never fails, when we trust Him, His peace never fails to appear.

The Little Foxes That Destroy Peace

Catch for us the foxes,
the little foxes that ruin the vineyards,
our vineyards that are in bloom.

Song of Solomon 2:15 NIV

It's the little foxes—or at least they start out small—that spoil our relationship with the Vine and blight our fruitfulness.

We know "big" sins—adultery, fornication, murder, robbery—put us at odds with God and destroy our peace of heart and mind. However, the little disobediences—like the milk teeth of young foxes gnawing on the tendrils of grapevines—nibble away our sweet peace.

By the same token, the world expects major problems—death, illness, job loss, wars, and other cataclysms—to disturb our lives and rob us of peace. But that isn't necessarily so. God's miraculous peace can be extended to us even at those times if we've maintained our connection to the Vine.

Here are seven "little foxes":

1. The times when we say "no" to God when we should run to obey.
2. The times when we say, "Just this once!" when we should say, "Never!"
3. The times when we let things slide or look the other direction.
4. The times when we color the truth or hide a lie.
5. The times when we take too much.
6. The times when we give too little.
7. The times when we say, "It's just the way I am!" or "I can't help it!"

We think those little sins shouldn't matter, but they do. And in the end, we wonder why our lives are barren, why we feel disconnected from God, and why we have no peace. But in order for the bloom of peace—that sweet relationship with God—to bear fruit, it has to stay connected to the Vine. Then the bloom and the fruit may be barraged by hail, snow, ice, and heat and still maintain their health, no matter how battered and bruised. But let the blooms and fruit lose connection with the life-giving Spirit, let the little foxes starting chewing on the stems that connect them to the Vine, and then almost immediately the flower and fruit will turn brown and wither.

> *Let me tell you about the Holy Spirit. He's very emotionally sensitive; He gets upset quickly. In fact, the image of the Holy Spirit in the Bible is that of a dove—a very sensitive bird. What makes the Holy Spirit sensitive? Sin. We grieve the Holy Spirit when, instead of moving toward righteousness, we entertain unrighteousness.*
>
> TONY EVANS

Check your life for those "little foxes." A lack of peace is symptomatic of bigger, deeper problems. Like a fever that indicates when the body is experiencing illness, disquiet is an indicator that something is wrong in your relationship with God.

How to Identify the "Little Foxes" That Steal Your Peace

Are you having a regular devotional time with the Lord? Not just a "hello!" yelled at God in passing as you rush through your life, but a time devoted to seeking His face?

Each Christian believer needs to spend time studying the Word and praying. Going to church, listening to Bible tapes, or praying in the car or at times when you are doing something else is fine—but be wary of the attitude that gives God only the leftovers of your day. As much as possible, your devotional time with God should be exclusively His.

- *Is God first? Or are there other things in life that are more important than God?* If God said to you in a loud, clear voice, "Sell all you have and give it to the poor," would you? If God undeniably said to you, "Quit your job and become a missionary," would you? If God clearly said to you, "Turn off the television and spend some time with Me," would you?

  If God is not first, He's not your God. If His way and will are not your primary concern, He may be your Insurance Policy, He may be your Santa-Claus-in-the-Sky, but He's not your God.

- *Is there secret sin in your life?* Are you hiding something from everybody else that is known only to you and God? You may think, "It's only a little sin. It's not hurting anyone but me," but when we are ashamed of ourselves before God, we tend to hide from His presence. Our communication with Him will thus be blocked—and our peace of mind will suffer.

- *Is there open sin in your life?* Just because something is condoned by the world doesn't mean that it is right. Lots of people steal, cheat, deceive, and bully. The world is full of people who use profanity, overeat, and gossip—but if you want peace, you'll have to leave behind anything that keeps you from experiencing God's peace.

- *Have you turned your back on God in any area?* It's surprising how many people think they can live like the devil while enjoying the privileges of the children of God. One of the first privileges they lose is peace. The pleasure of the sin may act as a temporary anesthetic to the pain of sin, but it is only a short-lived phenomenon. When it wears off, peace is not only gone, but torment takes its place.

- *Are you tolerating sin in your family that should be dealt with?* God holds you responsible to deal with rebellion and sin in a loving manner. Just because you are ignoring your responsibility does not mean you are exempt from it. Your lack of peace is God's goading you to deal with the problems in your own family.

- *Are you holding a grudge?* Maybe it's your own parents who have offended or hurt you. Maybe it's a friend or a business associate. Maybe the transgression was deliberate; perhaps it was accidental. We are told to forgive those who use us in a spiteful manner, to love and pray for our persecutors (Matt. 5:44). The forgiveness you extend is for your benefit as well because it opens the way for renewal and peace with God.

- *Are you a child of God?* Have you asked Jesus to forgive you of your sins? Have you asked Him to live His life through you? Have you asked His Holy Spirit to fill you? When you do, you will find true peace.

Joseph ran. His flying feet took him past the outskirts of Nazareth into the chalky hills. He didn't stop until he was miles out of town. Finally, he threw himself upon the rocky ground, heedless of the abrasions it made upon his skin.

It had been years since he had cried, but now tears spilled down his cheeks and into his beard. He hugged himself and moaned aloud. His surprise and anger went to the depth of his soul.

Of all the people who might have betrayed me, he thought in anguish, *I would never have guessed it would be Mary. Of all people, I thought her to be without guile.*

He had long loved Mary. He had dreamed of her being the mother of his children and the companion of his old age. He thought of her soul knit to his own. Now, he wondered if he had ever truly known her at all. He remembered her great modesty in keeping her face covered since the betrothal. She had taken great care never to be alone with him. Now, with bitterness, Joseph wondered with whom she had been alone. Joseph thought of the Arab camel traders and their bold ways with the village maidens. He thought of the few stray Roman soldiers in Nazareth on imperial business. He thought, too, of some of the slimy street boys who he knew spent their days in idle practices that inflamed passions. He bitterly wondered which of these had violated his bride. He would find Mary and make her tell. He would demand to know who he was and then Joseph would. . .do something! He could scarcely believe she might have done such a thing, but the fact remained that she was going to have a baby and that he, her espoused husband, had in no way been involved. Somehow, Joseph felt it would have been easier to accept if Mary had just come to him and told him of her whoredom. Joseph knew in his heart that he would have taken her for his wife if she had been with ten men and confessed it. He thought he knew her so well, but his only conclusion was that she had treated him entirely with falseness. To marry her now, Joseph felt, would be like taking a snake into his bosom.

Joseph began to walk. In the days when his grandfather kept many sheep, there was one special hillside where the pastureland was lush and the water always good, but Joseph liked that particular grazing field for another reason: Hidden amid the craggy, overgrown face of the hill was a dry cave. Joseph suddenly wanted to visit that childhood refuge. He skirted along the facade of the hill, looking for something to remind him where the cave was located. A few stones, loosened by his steps, slid down the embankment and disappeared behind some acacia scrub. The pebbles produced a hollow echo. Joseph pushed past the thorny branches of the bushes and slipped into the coolness of the cave.

Exhausted by his emotions, Joseph lay on the cave floor. Mary's face instantly appeared in his mind. The very thought of her made him grind his teeth with angry hurt and frustration. He wanted to marry the girl he once thought he knew, not this pregnant woman. His mind steadfastly refused to believe she had deceived him. It was so totally against her character that he could not believe the evidence. It simply had to be a misunderstanding. He would go to her and demand an explanation. She would tell him that everyone was mistaken. They were all wrong. She had been talking about someone else. Someone else was having a baby, not her, a different Mary. That was the explanation.

For a moment, his mind rested in fantasy and denial. He lay on his back, his hands under his head and smiled at the roof of the cave. His Mary was innocent and still a virgin. He had to get this straightened out before the entire village heard of it.

But in his heart, he knew better. Like a huge boulder, the awful truth remained: Mary was pregnant. He knew his family would demand a divorce and have Mary stoned. A pregnant espoused wife would be very bad for business. After all, who could trust a man who would violate the agreements of a marriage contract for a few seconds of passion? But he did not want Mary stoned. It was his right, once the child was born, to have his honor avenged and his name cleared, but that would involve the death of this woman that he loved regardless of what she had done.

His imagination saw Mary's oval face composed, but her expressive eyes wide with fear as the villagers, led by rabbis, shoved her through the streets and out of the village to the steep hills surrounding Nazareth. There was one cliff, just to the southwest of town, that bore the distinction of being the stoning ground. His mind saw Mary atop the cliff assuming that humble but dignified stance of hers while the rabbi read the charge of adultery and urged her to repent before she died. Mary turned to quietly face the condemning crowd, but somehow his imagination could not make Mary guilty.

She just looked at the people and never said a word. One by one, the jeering crowd was silenced. Even the rabbis looked uncertain. They whispered together, then summoned Joseph to the front. As the wronged party, he would be required to throw the first stone. Someone handed him a large chunk of limestone. His arms held the rock above his head for what seemed like an eternity. "Stone her! Stone her! In the name of Jehovah God, stone her!"

Mary was looking at him, her eyes reaching into his, her mind and soul touching his. They spoke: *I am not guilty*. He could not throw the rock. He would divorce her, but no matter what anyone else said, he would not take her life.

The blackness of despair settled over him. Like a disappointed child, he cried until he had no more tears, then gradually fell into a deep sleep. For a time, he slept heavily and dreamless. Then he felt his mind awaken while his body slumbered on. Suddenly, he found himself suffused in bright beams that were not merely light but a person. He covered his face in fright. Then the voice commanded him with such authority not to fear that he stopped quaking and tried to look through the shine at the one before him.

Joseph had never seen anything like him before. The being spoke, his voice blending into a harmony of music.

"Joseph, son of David! Do not be afraid to take Mary home as your wife because what is conceived in her is from the Holy Spirit. She will give birth to a son, and you are to give Him the name Jesus, because He will save His people from their sins."

In an instant, Joseph's body was awake. He climbed out of the cave and sat against the hill with the sunshine full upon his face. He felt completely at peace and strangely excited. He was amazed by the dream almost to the point of shouting. He realized that those few short sentences spoken to him by the angel would not only change his life but the future of the whole of Jewish race. The long-awaited Messiah was about to be born. He would see the salvation of Israel. Indeed, he would participate in it! The Son of the Most High God! Born into the world, into his home via his little Mary! He reran the words of the angel again and again, gathering strength from each rehearsal.

Mary was still his faithful friend and could still be his wife.

He knew he needed to make the necessary arrangements for Mary to come to his home. There was no reason to put it off any longer. He could spend every spare moment with her. He could hold her hand and touch her face, although he knew no other intimacy was possible at the present, and strangely enough, not even desired. Together, they could plan their home and make arrangements for this wondrous Child that was to be born to them.

His Mary, chosen to be the mother of the Messiah! It seemed so right and natural he wondered how he had ever thought differently. He would be the guardian and teacher of this remarkable little boy. He didn't feel at all qualified; God would show him what to do. In the meantime, he had good news, and he wanted to shout it from the housetops of Nazareth and whisper it softly in Mary's ear.

One common mistake we make is dwelling on the negative. We preoccupy ourselves with our own faults or the faults of others. We look for and expect only the bad in people and situations generally. It is not surprising that we find exactly what we are seeking. Such negative mediating yields only chaos and self-destruction. Meditate, instead, on Christ.

DR. ROBERT S. MASERONI

Uprooting the Discord

Fresh out of college with no debt, no money, a new baby girl, and lots of energy, my husband and I bought an abandoned house situated on some country acreage. This was to be our Garden of Eden, our haven of self-sufficiency. However, it was also where we learned the hard, callous-producing truth about the curse God put on the soil, "It will produce thorns and thistles for you. . . . By the sweat of your brow you will eat your food"!

The frame and brick of the house were solid and showed graceful promise, but beyond that, it needed everything—plumbing, electricity, insulation, new plaster. The yard, on the other hand, already had everything—plus! In addition to a large, dilapidated barn, outbuildings, and old foundations, the entire two and a half acres were littered with plain junk. Not good junk, mind you, but old, awful, rusty hunks of pure, unadulterated junk—old Cadillac chassis, doorless refrigerators, rusted-out water heaters, and many more treasures of equal or lesser value. Scattered throughout all of this rubbish were straggly cherry and mulberry trees. Lavishly festooned with poison ivy and thistles, they grew up like crowded, forbidding fortresses guarding the junk, greatly impeding our progress as we cleaned the yard.

In order to move the junk and mow the yard, the thickets

had to be grubbed out. At first glance, it seemed like a brilliant idea to set fire to the yard and burn off the underbrush to facilitate junk removal. Fortunately, we had second thoughts about the whole process because burning poison ivy throws its sap into the air. Whatever the smoke touches—be it skin, eyes, lungs, or clothing—is then covered by the miserable, itch-producing poison of the weed! The result would have been a two-week or ten-day foretaste of hell! Spraying the poison ivy with weed killer was not a totally satisfactory option, either. The herbicide would kill the plant and its roots, but dead or alive, poison ivy is still poison ivy and every bit as nasty.

There remained only one solution: With a knitted ski mask covering my face, rubber gloves on my hands, and every possible square inch of skin covered, I armed myself with a scythe and a hoe and ridded the yard of this form of the curse. The plants had to be yanked up by their roots, wrapped in plastic bags, and hauled off the property before we could get to the work of removing the ugly but less menacing junk in the yard.

Anarchy of the soul—the lack of peace—has a lot in common with poison ivy and brambles. Strife grows chaotically around the sin and bad habits in our lives, entangling, tripping, and confusing us, hampering our ability to deal with the obvious problems. We want to get rid of the big ugly junk in our lives, but it is woven tightly to our hearts by the poisons and thistles of selfishness. These weeds seem to be mere nuisances;

but when we take them on, we find ourselves handling stubbornly entrenched thoughts and attitudes that aren't going to give way without a fight! What can we do with those torments, real yet intangible, that keep us uneasy and afraid, unable to move the big, rusty problems in our lives?

When we surrender our problems to Jesus, when we allow Him full access to our hearts, He pulls the "poison ivy" out by the roots. And then He whispers, "Peace!"

When we trust Jesus in our situations, we become effective tools in His hands. Then He can use us to rid our lives of those things that disturb our peace of mind. When we resist Him, it is like a rake or hoe running away from the Gardener. When we doubt Him, it is like a garden tool suddenly going limp. But when we place ourselves in His capable hands and are obedient to His will—even when we don't understand exactly what we are to do—He can move through us to work on our situations. Then we will truly experience God's peace.

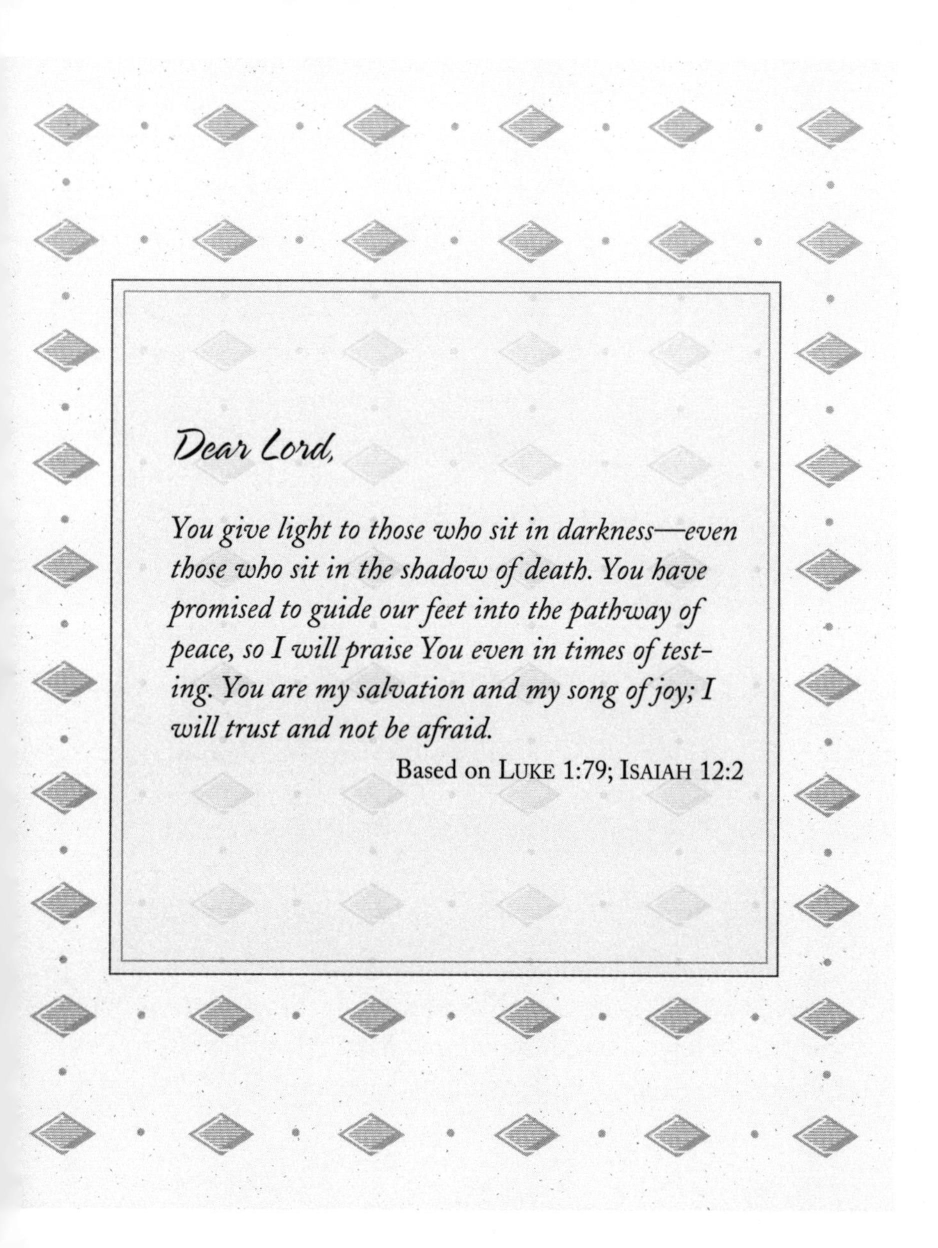

Dear Lord,

You give light to those who sit in darkness—even those who sit in the shadow of death. You have promised to guide our feet into the pathway of peace, so I will praise You even in times of testing. You are my salvation and my song of joy; I will trust and not be afraid.

Based on LUKE 1:79; ISAIAH 12:2

Chapter 5

A Harvest of Peace During Troubled Times

For he is our peace. . . .

EPHESIANS 2:14

Now the Lord of peace himself give you peace always by all means. 2 THESSALONIANS 3:16

Here is an odd, paradoxical thought: Sometimes peace is only birthed by force. Force is sometimes required to contain aggression or discipline a rebellious child. Sometimes force is required to right wrongs, and sometimes God has to force us to turn our attention to Him so He can bring peace to our souls.

On the Stormy Waters

(Based on Matthew 14:22–34)

Even experienced fishermen shuddered when the wind howled out of the mountains and onto the sea. Then the waves became choppy and unpredictable; men who worked these waters all their lives knew to haul their sails and make for harbor. But sometimes—and this night was one of them—the high seas and gusts would not permit the sailors to gain the shore.

The small boat circled the middle of the sea, an eerie spot, wild, unsettled, dangerous—and according to some reports—haunted. In watery graves below lay hundreds, if not thousands, of the sailors' fellow fishermen waiting for them to join them, their boats reduced to waterlogged splinters, their bones picked clean by the same denizens of the deep they had come to harvest.

By three o'clock in the morning, as a false dawn dimly lit the sky, the men had been pulling on the oars for hours against the wind. No nearer shore, shelter, or sanctuary; exhaustion was setting in. Then one man caught a glimpse of something unsettling on the seas.

For a few moments, a trough obscured his vision, and while he waited for the lift of the next wave, he pondered whether he was seeing things. When the wave lofted them upward, he looked steadily over his shoulder. There it was again!

He gave a shriek of terror and pointed as the boat was again swallowed by a curl of water. "What?" someone shouted above the wind's howl. His question was answered as the boat crested the wave; every man in the boat saw the phantom, a dead man risen from the deep, walking on the water toward the boat. "A ghost!"

It was true, then! The sea was indeed haunted—and unless God spared them by some miraculous means, they were all going to die. Gripped by terror, they rowed frantically, their strokes uncoordinated, panic-stricken, and fruitless. Each wave revealed a truth more horrible than the last: The ghost was gaining on them.

Then a voice rang out over the storm: "Take courage, men! It's I! Don't be afraid!"

The men paused midstroke and stared at one another, eyes wide with fear and hope. The voice sounded like Jesus, but how could it be He? This creature was walking on the water! It could not be a flesh-and-blood man.

"It's a trick!" someone hissed. "The ghost mimics the

voice of the Master!"

A man of action, Peter could not sit in the boat and wait to see if it was a demon approaching or their Savior. He would go to the Master—or drown in the effort. "If it is You, Lord," he shouted, "tell me to come to You on the water."

"Come!" rang out the voice above the roar of wind and wave.

Peter threw his leg over the stern.

"No!" shouted his brother Andrew. "Don't go! You'll drown!"

Peter shook off his brother and stepped out. Although he had developed sea legs as a toddler, he still needed to adjust to the rise and fall of the stormy waves. Nevertheless, Peter was filled with a wild exhilaration. Sometimes he could clearly see Jesus walking toward him, sometimes not.

True dawn was not far off now, but the wind off the mountains grew stronger. The waves dashed higher, wilder, more unpredictable; engulfed among them, Peter totally lost sight of the Master. "Jesus?" he called. He scanned the undulating swells, but for all he could tell, he was alone. He looked behind him for the boat, but it, too, had disappeared. *What am I doing out here?* he asked himself, suddenly doubting his sanity. *This must be a madman's nightmare! There was no Jesus on the sea. I am alone and a fool!*

Immediately, he began to sink, water washing over his head, filling his lungs. He coughed violently, but he had only enough breath for a whisper. "Lord! Save me!" he cried out hoarsely, flailing wildly, foaming whitecaps rolling over his head.

The wave dropped, and instantly Jesus was there. His warm hand caught Peter's shivering arm and pulled him out of the pounding waters. "Why did you doubt?" Jesus asked him.

At that moment, his hand held tightly and warmly in Jesus' hand, Peter didn't know why either. Now, with Jesus' strong arm around him, the heaving waves were nothing but a nuisance. They stepped over each wave until the boat came into view.

The men were still wildly and fruitlessly wielding the oars so Jesus and Peter were able to come within a dozen yards before they were spotted. Then the men watched their approach, stunned and disbelieving, right up to the moment when Peter and Jesus stepped over the rocking gunwale. Immediately, suddenly, even before they were seated, the wind died. The once restless sea lay smooth and shining as the first blush of the sun's rays tinted the sky.

When You Are Battling a Storm

- . . .look for Jesus in it. He's there somewhere, and if you can tear your eyes off the waves, you'll spot Him coming to your aid.

- . . .worship Him as Master of the sea. If all you look at is the storm, it becomes your focus, the thing of utmost importance to your mind; if you worship Him as God, you will find that God does indeed dwell in the praises of His people.

- . . .do what Jesus says even if He commands you to get out of your safety zone, leave your security, and walk on the water. If He says you can do it, do it.

- . . .keep Jesus in your vision. No matter how big the problems are that are approaching you, no matter how threatening they appear, keep Him in your sight. If a problem temporarily eclipses Him from view, don't assume that He's abandoned you. He's still there—even when you can't see Him.

- . . .if you get into waters over your head, call for Jesus' help. He'll be there.

- . . .walk with His hand in yours. Cling to Him. He's promised never to leave or forsake you. He understands storms and how to deal with them.

- . . .when He is walking with you, impossible feats

are suddenly possible; but don't forget that it isn't you, your righteousness, your faith, or anything else about you that makes them possible—it's only the saving grace of Jesus.

- . . .expect that He'll bring peace. Jesus is the Prince of Peace. When you invite Him to reign in your life, He automatically brings peace.

As on Galilee

I wish that I had been with Him on stormy Galilee
When with a quiet word of peace He hushed the restless sea.
And yet I know I need not go to distant ages dim
To see the stormy winds of life and waves obeying Him.
When summoned now, He speaks again and bids the wild winds cease,
And in our hearts the winds go down and waves are hushed in peace!

ARTHUR WALLACE

Peace Against All Reason

When Diana's ex-husband Charles kidnapped their ten-year-old son Larry, she had doubted she would ever get him back. "Just a month before Charles took him," said Diana, "Larry was arrested for possession of cocaine. Of course, I was stunned! How could my little boy have cocaine? He tested negative for consumption, so I knew he was carrying the cocaine for someone else. The police knew it, too."

Diana questioned Larry closely, and although the boy would not directly admit it, she suspected Larry was acting as a "mule" or a courier for her ex-husband. She resisted allowing Charles his one-month summer visit with Larry because of her suspicions, but the court ordered her to turn Larry over to his father. "At that time, my ex-husband and his father were highly influential local officials," said Diana. "The police were afraid to cross them, and Charles apparently had incriminating evidence on some of the people in the judicial system. I had been worried for a while that Charles would kidnap Larry —if for no other reason than just to keep him quiet."

When Charles did flee the state with Larry, Diana found herself in a terrifying and frustrating position. "I couldn't get anybody to cooperate with me so I could find Larry," she said. "No one else understood why it was dangerous for Charles to have Larry. I knew he needed to keep Larry out of state so he wouldn't testify against him."

If it hadn't been for the Lord, Diana would have fallen apart. "Sometimes I couldn't pray. I was so wrapped up in my own emotions and distraught," said Diana. "And although I couldn't share the details of Larry's situation, I had Christian friends who prayed. I definitely had prayer cover!"

Diana says that Larry's return is a living example of the parable of the unjust judge who was besieged by the poor widow (Luke 18:1–8). "I just kept after the police and legal system and nagged them to death until they acted for me. They said to me what the unjust judge said to the widow, 'We'll give you justice if you will go away!' Through one miracle after another, Diana was able to locate Larry and have him returned to her.

However, Larry still had to face juvenile court and the charges against him. "On the day we were to go to court, I was sitting on the front steps of my house beseeching the Lord for help," said Diana. "I knew Larry would have to testify and that all of Charles's family would be there. (Charles was still hiding out of state.) Larry would be under tremendous pressure to shield his dad and to lie, but I had told him over and over that as a Christian, he had to tell the truth.

"I asked the Lord, 'How can I console this child? What can I do for my son?' Then the Lord spoke to my heart: 'Think like a child,' He said to me.

"At those words, I just wept. My concerns were far less than my son's. He was facing his father's family and a judge, but as a little boy, he had concerns like, 'What if I have to go to the bathroom in the courtroom? If they send me to jail, will there be heat? Will my mother still love me?'

"After the Lord spoke to me, I was able to let go of my fears and be the mother of my child and meet his needs. My mind had been filled with last-minute legal details, but I was able to shove all those things aside. I woke him up and said, 'Let's go for a bike ride!' " For the next two hours, they were able to forget all about going to court and just enjoy the birds and sunshine.

"This was the most loving thing I could have done for him," Diana said. "After all, if you were a child who feared you were going to jail, wouldn't you want to take a bike ride? This bike ride was the beginning of a new trust between Larry and me, a trust that had been degraded by his father."

Larry was truthful in court, and he was sentenced to time in a juvenile facility and a year of counseling. While Charles's family protested, threatened, and objected, the police snapped the handcuffs on Larry to lead him away.

"I did not fall apart," Diana said. "I felt the Lord's arms around me. I knew He was there. I didn't even have to ask. Does a baby feel her mother's arms around her when that's all she's ever known? God just kept His arms around me and I just lay back into them."

At the same time, her eyes were opened to see her son's pain. "Normally, I would have been sobbing in a tissue, but when God opens your eyes to see the pain of other people, you don't hurt so much for yourself; you feel for them." She also saw something else. "When the police handcuffed Larry to take him to the detention facility, Charles's father tried to influence the uniformed officer to go easier on Larry, but the officer said to Charles's dad, 'You have no authority here! Leave the courtroom!' I thought, *Isn't that what we're supposed to tell Satan? 'You have no authority here!'* "

Diana now has full custody of Larry while his father is only allowed supervised visits. Charles will not return to the state because of outstanding warrants, however, nor does he ever call Larry. For the first time, Diana feels that Larry is safe from his father's reach and influence. She revels in the peace of God that has kept her soul and mind through the times of tempest.

> *Be still, and know that I am God: I will be exalted among the heathen, I will be exalted in the earth.*
>
> PSALM 46:10

Abide with Me

Abide with me, fast falls the eventide:
The darkness deepens, Lord, with me abide;
When other helpers fail and comforts flee,
Help of the helpless, O abide with me.

HENRY F. LYTE

Worry does not empty
tomorrow of its sorrow;
it empties today of its strength.

CORRIE TEN BOOM

You will keep in perfect peace
him whose mind is steadfast,
because he trusts in you.

ISAIAH 26:3 NIV

Peace, Trouble, and the God of Goodness

"True peace of mind comes from being able to accept whatever comes your way from the hand of God, regardless of how unfair, unpredictable, and irrational it seems now," Dave said. Dave was clearly taught this lesson when his son David was about two years old.

"My neighbor and I were talking in the front yard while David played at our feet. We stepped into the garage for only a second to look at something, but when we came out, David was nowhere to be seen. Somewhere in the distance, I heard this little yowl, then out of the corner of my eye, I saw my neighbor leap over the fence separating our yards."

Behind the fence, a life-or-death drama was taking place. The neighbor had caught a tiny glimpse of David as he disappeared under his pool covering; the "yowl" was the last noise he made just before he sank to the bottom. Galvanized into action, the neighbor cleared the fence and leaped into the pool, rescuing tiny David in the nick of time.

But the story was not over. A week later, Dave was out in his yard when he spotted a helicopter flying low over the trees of their subdivision. As he watched, it landed about a mile away, near a group of rescue vehicles and police cars. Later, Dave discovered that the same neighbor who had rescued his son now had a tragedy of his own—his nineteen-year-old son had been hit on a bicycle, and he was being life-flighted to a hospital.

The boy survived but remained a quadriplegic. The pool that so nearly claimed the life of little David was drained, and an addition was tacked on the side of the house to care for the profoundly handicapped young man. "Every day when I come out of my house," Dave said, "I see that addition. And every day I thank God that I receive good things from Him I don't deserve.

"Some people think peace of mind means God will do what they want or fix some bad thing the way they want Him to. But peace of mind is accepting whatever comes from the hand of God—obvious blessing or a blessing disguised as a bad thing.

"My neighbor did a good thing—he rescued my drowning son. He received what seems like a bad thing in return—a quadriplegic son. But we thank God when something good happens—even though we don't deserve it—while we're pretty quick to accuse God of unfairness when something bad happens. True peace of mind is being able to accept whatever happens, knowing God loves me and He is in control. Even if I don't understand what has happened, I'll wait and ask Him about it face-to-face."

Sometimes we become rebellious and hard. We stop praying. We quit church or we question the whole matter of religion or, if we are of another temperament, we may pine away, and just give up. Jesus said, "Men ought always to pray, and not to faint." There is no sublimer sight than that of the soul who, bruised and crushed, still prays on, trusts on, fights on, leaving all doubts and all unanswered prayers before the throne of God, to be dealt with as God Himself wills. JAMES LUDWELL DAVIS

The Blossom of Peace in Pain

Marilu said that leaving her adopted identical twin sons behind when she left her husband, Mike, was one of the hardest things she ever had to do.

"Their mother died when they were born; they were thirteen months old when we married. Mike said I could adopt them after the wedding, but as soon as I confronted him about his alcoholism, he changed his mind."

A workaholic as well as an alcoholic, Mike was seldom home so the boys became Marilu's world. She soon gave birth to two more children and plunged herself into the demands of rearing preschoolers. "Mike was a good husband and father when he was sober," said Marilu, "but drunk, he was a demon! He was always endangering the children. Once, when he was so drunk that he couldn't stand, he took them on a wild boat ride. The kids were two, three, and five, at the time. They didn't have on life jackets or anything. It could have been a terrible tragedy."

On the heels of the boat incident, Mike had several auto accidents with the children, all due to his drinking. Then his careless behavior turned violent, and he began to beat Marilu. In this rapidly deteriorating situation, Marilu grabbed the children and left. "I had committed myself to all of these children. I could not leave them where they would be in danger."

She soon found out, however, she could not keep the twins. Although she charged Mike with child endangerment, because she had no blood ties, her lawyers said, "You either take the twins back or be charged with kidnapping." Reluctantly, she relinquished the twins.

As she drove away, she began to sob. "I completely crumbled," she recalled. "Separating from them gave me more pain and fear than I had ever suffered!" Another week and a half did not lessen the grief. Barely able to function, Marilu knew she had to pull herself together somehow for the other two children. "I prayed, 'Oh Lord, I cannot survive this! Can you take this pain from me? I have two children left, but I can't even take care of them!'

"The Lord gave me a promise that night from Isaiah 54:13: 'All your sons will be taught by the LORD, and great will be your children's peace' (NIV). I threw myself on that verse and clung to it. I knew the twins would be safe and that someday God would restore our relationship.

"Just like that, the excruciating pain stopped. I dried my tears, and I slept. I missed the twins terribly, but I didn't have that terrible grief. Six months later, the grief did come back, but I was able to handle it then. By that time, God had given me a Christ-centered support system."

Over the next year, she began to think of God as her mate. "To not be part of a 'we' was painful," she said, "until someone pointed out that the only true 'we' was God and me. From then on, when I said, 'we,' I meant God and me."

Over the next ten years, Marilu longed for her twin sons. Then when they were sixteen, the boys began calling her. She said that, today, her relationship with them is completely restored and that she has had the privilege of leading both boys—now men—to the Lord. "I never doubted for a moment that God would restore my family. He gave me assurance and peace."

Reaping the Fruit of Peace in the Battle Zone

Here are a few suggestions to bring God's peace into a troubled setting:

- Seek peace, not revenge. Paul addressed a similar situation when he wrote, "Do not repay anyone evil for evil. . . . If it is possible, as far as it depends on you, live at peace with everyone. Do not take revenge, my friends, but leave room for God's wrath, for it is written: 'It is mine to avenge; I will repay,' says the Lord." (Romans 12:17–19 NIV)

- Seek reconciliation rather than a temper display. The old saying, "The wind of anger blows out the lamp of intelligence," is very true. The Bible states it another way: "In your anger do not sin." (Ephesians 4:26 NIV) Unfairness, dishonesty, cruelty, and other sins against people should make you angry, but don't let that anger sweep away your ability to bring about a sound settlement.

- Spread encouragement, not gossip. It is hard for some people to keep their mouths shut when they know some scrap of scandal, and if you are one of those, look at yourself every day in the mirror and pray, "LORD, set a watch on my mouth. 'Deliver my soul, O LORD, from lying lips, and from a deceitful tongue' (Psalm 120:2)—especially my own!" When someone tells you something, unless he is doing something illegal or life threatening, keep it to yourself. The only other exception to this is if someone tells you something good about another person; then pass it on. This will help keep the peace in whatever situation you are in.

There is an extra advantage to this: When you keep confidences, people know it and trust you.

- Seek solutions rather than complaining. This can be hard. Sometimes, your boss or a person in authority can be a real jerk, and you want to share his or her latest outrage with your co-sufferers—but don't do it. Paul wrote: "Do not let any unwholesome talk come out of your mouths, but only what is helpful for building others up according to their needs, that it may benefit those who listen." (Ephesians 4:29 NIV)

- Seek sound judgment rather than exaggerating the situation. In a troubled situation, people sometimes lose sound judgment because they are lying to themselves about the problem. They'll say to themselves, "This is terrible!" when in reality, it is only frustrating. Then, because they have stretched the problem all out of proportion, they think they have to find a huge solution. They find themselves discouraged, frightened, and unable to deal with the situation because they have lost perspective.

- Analyze the problem honestly. In looking for solutions, speak what you believe to be the opposing party's view. In other words, you might say, "As I understand your position, you believe that I should do things this way. Is that correct?" Always ask for clarification of the other person's position and then restate it to be certain you understand. When he agrees with your statement of his position, then state yours. Misunderstandings—if your problem is a misunderstanding—can be cleared up this way. Even if you and your opposition have diametrically opposing positions, at least you'll have a clear understanding of how he feels.

- Keep your goal in mind. Your goal must always be to bring glory to God in any situation. How can this best be accomplished? Do you have to apologize to someone? Do you have to take a backseat and allow someone else to lead? Do you need to swallow an insult or a slight? Do you need to bless rather than curse? The writer of Hebrews put it succinctly: "Let us throw off everything that hinders and the sin that so easily entangles, and let us run with perseverance the race marked out for us. Let us fix our eyes on Jesus, the author and perfecter of our faith, who for the joy set before him endured the cross, scorning its shame, and sat down at the right hand of the throne of God. Consider him who endured such opposition from sinful men, so that you will not grow weary and lose heart." (Hebrews 12:1–3 NIV)

Dear Lord,

Even as You form the light and create the darkness, You make peace. Give me peace in my heart, soul, and life. The peace You give is not like the world gives, but is a quiet resting in You. I am thankful for the blessings You have sent me, but when bad things happen, I tend to blame You. You cause the sun to rise on the evil and the good, however, and You send rain on the righteous and unrighteous. You are a good God and mean only good for me, despite how I view my circumstances. Forgive me for my doubts.

You sent Jesus to give light to me when I

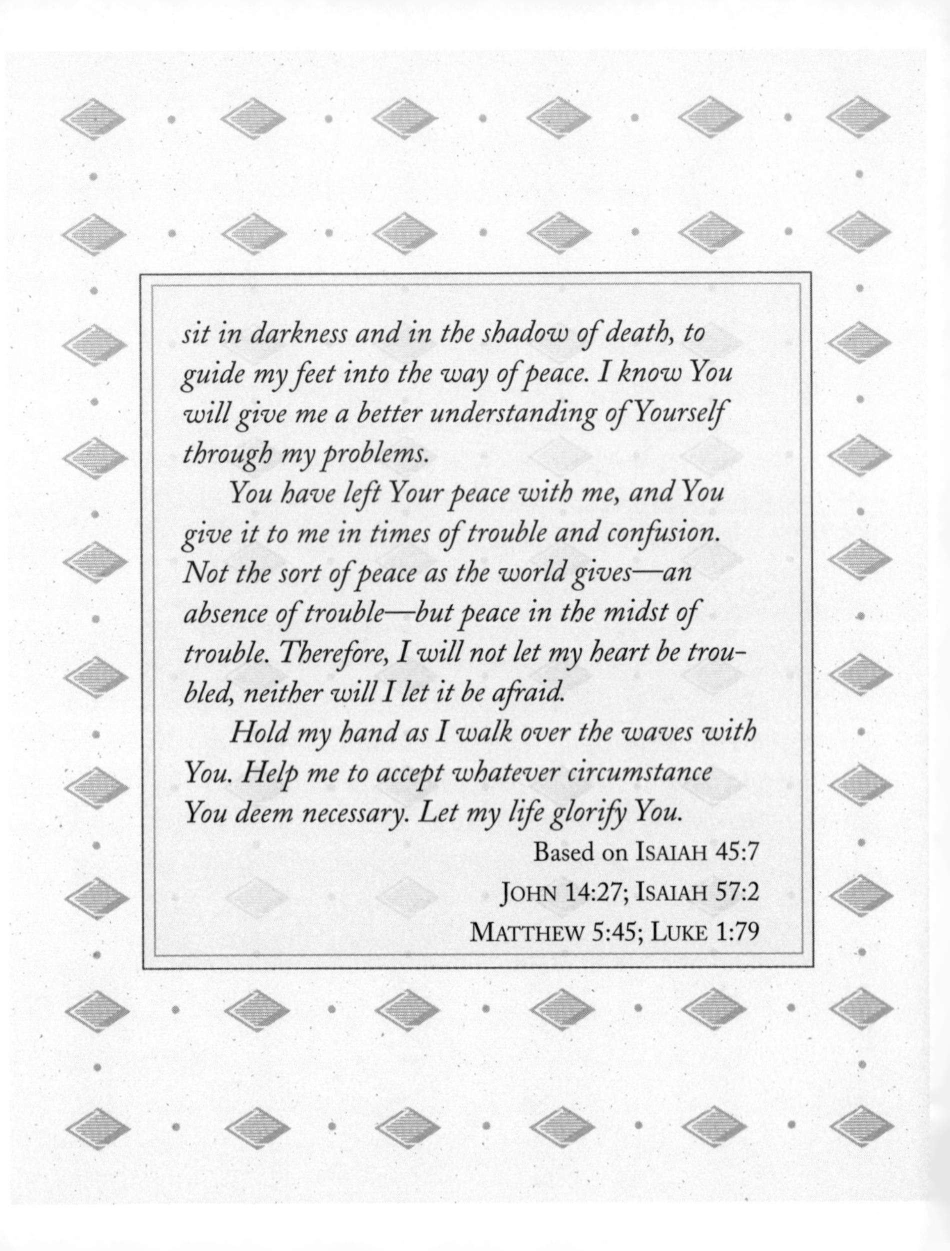

sit in darkness and in the shadow of death, to guide my feet into the way of peace. I know You will give me a better understanding of Yourself through my problems.

You have left Your peace with me, and You give it to me in times of trouble and confusion. Not the sort of peace as the world gives—an absence of trouble—but peace in the midst of trouble. Therefore, I will not let my heart be troubled, neither will I let it be afraid.

Hold my hand as I walk over the waves with You. Help me to accept whatever circumstance You deem necessary. Let my life glorify You.

Based on ISAIAH 45:7

JOHN 14:27; ISAIAH 57:2

MATTHEW 5:45; LUKE 1:79

Chapter 6

A Peacemaker's Seeds of Righteousness

Blessed are the peacemakers:
for they shall be called
the children of God.

MATTHEW 5:9

But the wisdom that comes
from heaven is first of all pure;
then peace loving, considerate,
submissive, full of mercy
and good fruit,
impartial and sincere.
Peacemakers who sow in peace
raise a harvest of righteousness.

JAMES 3:17–18 NIV

William Law's first rule of life:

To fix it deep in my mind that I have but one business upon my hands, to seek for eternal happiness by doing the will of God.

Weed Seeds or Roses?

It was a sweet November–November romance. Clete was a bachelor farmer that no one thought would ever get married; Bessie was the widow of an old buddy of Clete's who lived in town. Their marriage was a surprise to everyone, but once the knot was tied, everyone agreed that they made the cutest couple.

Ever since he got back from the military after World War II, Clete ran the family farm with strict precision. The entire operation was a model of efficiency. Every building was neatly painted; and the equipment, no matter its vintage, looked like it had just been driven off the showroom floor. Even the crops and animals stood at attention. Driving along the country roads, you could distinguish Clete's fields from his neighbor's, so remarkable were they for their straight furrows and clean rows. Most of all, Clete was fanatical about weeds. He absolutely hated them and killed them with every method possible. He sprayed them, mowed them, plowed them, and when all else failed, hacked them out with the hoe —anything to keep them from taking root on his farm.

The farm and agrarian life were new and novel to Bessie. She grew up in the city and came to the small nearby town with her first husband. She'd never so much as had a garden. But in a wise, albeit old-fashioned, attempt to be a good wife, she thought if Clete tilled the soil, she should too. So under his careful tutelage, they tilled up an area just behind the house and sowed it with vegetables. In the evenings, Bessie and Clete hoed around the tender plants and talked over the day. Then spring planting and cultivation shifted into high gear. Weather permitting, Clete was in the fields from crack of dawn to long after sunset, leaving the garden and house to Bessie's care.

Bessie was quite proud of her little vegetable patch. She'd picked the first peas and zucchini and spotted some embryonic tomatoes and green beans. Although she liked the tidy garden, she longed for a few flowers to soften the austere lines. Then one day, driving back from town, she spotted some delicate flowers growing alongside the road. She had no idea of the plant's real name, but because of its lacey appearance, she nicknamed it the "doily plant," dug some up, and took them home. Now, she, too, felt like a farmer. She planted them the entire length of the garden, and lying in bed at night with the bone-tired Clete, bragged happily to him about her "doily plants." He'd love them when they bloomed, she said.

Clete wasn't exactly listening. He heard Bessie—more or less—but his farm work totally occupied his mind. Had he been listening, he might have realized that Bessie had planted Queen Anne's Lace (also known as wild carrot) across his beloved farm—a lovely, but an exceptionally pervasive scourge to farmers.

So the seeds were set: Bessie expected to pleasantly surprise Clete; Clete wasn't paying attention. Then one hot morning in late June, Clete stepped out on the porch to enjoy a bit of respite and spotted Bessie's plants blooming in their full glory. He was speechless with horror. He had spent years eradicating Queen Anne's Lace off his property; now his bride was planting it!

Bessie slipped out on the porch behind him, waiting for his rapturous approval. "What do you think of my doily plants?" she asked, basking in anticipatory glory.

"Those aren't plants!" Clete gasped. "They're weeds! They've got to be chopped down before they seed themselves all over the farm!"

"They most certainly are not weeds!" Bessie sputtered angrily. "They're flowers. Can't you see that they're blooming?"

When the shock passed for both of them, Clete explained the problem with the doily plants. Certain plants, like these, defeat the purpose of farming, he told her. They scatter seeds willy-nilly, and once established, they're the very dickens to grub out. That's why they're called "weeds." They grow uncontrollably.

Eventually, Clete and Bessie had a good laugh, then grabbed the hoe, and chopped out the doily plants while discussing where to plant rose bushes.

The Bible warns us to guard our hearts with all diligence, like Clete did his farm, and to be careful of the seeds we plant there, because like a garden, the harvest we reap from our hearts feeds our ability to live. Out of our heart comes our response to the issues of life. At first glance, some thoughts and attitudes appear benign and attractive—like doily plants. Unfortunately, they produce a noxious crop with an outcome that is hard to control and wreaks havoc.

The Bible suggests a crop of helpful attitudes to plant. When we plant these, the peace of God stands like a sentinel over our hearts (Philippians 4:7).

> *Be careful for nothing; but in every thing by prayer and supplication with thanksgiving let your requests be made known unto God. And the peace of God, which passeth all understanding, shall keep your hearts and minds through Christ Jesus.*
>
> *Finally, brethren, whatsoever things are true, whatsoever things are honest, whatsoever things are just, whatsoever things are pure, whatsoever things are lovely,*

whatsoever things are of good report; if there be any virtue, and if there be any praise, think on these things. Those things, which you have both learned, and received, and heard, and seen in me, do: and the God of peace shall be with you.

PHILIPPIANS 4:6–9

- *Seeds of Truth*—Take care of exaggeration, half-truths, embellishments, boasting. Don't permit yourself to shade—or even tint—the truth because while the truth will set you free, falsehoods will ensnare you. Lies may falsely comfort you for a while but truth will give you true peace.

There are things which are true. Many things in this world are deceptive and illusory, promising what they can never perform, offering a specious peace and happiness which they can never supply. A man should always set his thoughts on things which will not let him down.

WILLIAM BARCLAY

- *Seeds of Honesty*—Other translations of this verse interpret the word as "honorable" or "worthy." Often we justify participating in a practice or activity with the question, "What's wrong with it?" when the question we should be asking is: "What's right with it? Is this a practice that is helpful to my friendship with God? Is this an activity that will bring me turmoil or peace? Is this the activity for the son or daughter of the King of Kings?"

Human beings need both practice and study over time to become persons of integrity and effective goodwill. And until they have achieved such a state, they may do all sorts of things that prudence tells them had better be concealed.

WILLIAM J. BENNETT

- *Seeds of Justice*—Jesus said, "Render unto Caesar the things that are Caesar's, and unto God the things that are God's." Don't allow yourself to become riddled by worry because you have not cared for your responsibilities to God and man. The just person is reliable and dependable. He will discover that justice grows peace of mind.

- *Seeds of Purity*—There are some who go out of their way to look for impurity to fondle in their hearts. There are some who can find perversion in the most innocent phrase or action. They are looking for a way to scratch an indefinable itch, and by the search, make it fester that much more. The result is a choking weed that robs them of their lives of vitality and peace. Those who plant purity can find joy and peace in every area.

One is one's own teacher, trainer, coach, and disciplinarian. It is an odd sort of relationship, paradoxical in its own way, and many of us don't handle it very well. There is much unhappiness and personal distress in the world because of failures to control tempers, appetites, passions, and impulses. "Oh, if only I had stopped myself" is an all too familiar refrain. WILLIAM J. BENNETT

- *Seeds of Loveliness*—Winsome, attractive, the ability to elicit love from others—all are interpretations of loveliness. Christians should actively seek to be the type of persons who attract people to themselves so they can point them to God.

There are those whose minds are so set on vengeance and punishment that they call forth bitterness and fear in others. There are those whose minds are so set on criticism and rebuke that they call forth resentment in others. The mind of the Christian is set on the lovely things—kindness, sympathy, forbearance—so he is a winsome person, whom to see is to love. WILLIAM BARCLAY

- *Seeds That Are of Good Report*—The best interpretation of this phrase is that the believer is urged to think thoughts that are fit for God to think. Before admitting something into our lives, the criterion should be: Would Jesus think or say these things? Would Jesus go there and engage in that activity? These should be the standard for speech and conduct for the believer. Activities that are offensive to the Holy Spirit cause separation from God and discord in the soul.

- *Seeds of Virtue*—Moral education—the training of the heart and mind toward the excellent—involves many facets. Some of it is learning the rules; much of it is developing good habits—Bible reading, prayer, church attendance, honesty, self-discipline, responsibility, a good work ethic, and so forth. These excellent habits pave the road for a peaceful, godly way to live.

- *Praiseworthy Seeds*—This involves good habits, clean thoughts, and positive actions. These are the habits of a person who will win the commendation of men and a hearty "well done" from God.

Wisdom from above is not cultivated by man. It is seeded by God, blooms with peace, and bears righteousness.

A Guide to the Seeds of Peaceable Wisdom

I once saw an advertisement for a tree that was billed to bear five different types of fruit. I was intrigued by the prospect, but it was an expensive tree, and while I knew this marvel of horticulture was achieved through grafting, I had my doubts about how healthy such a tree would be. I thought it might be weak because of all of the grafts.

Like the aforementioned tree, wisdom from God is multi-fruited—but it is abundantly healthy and strong! Planted by the Holy Spirit through a peacemaking individual, peaceable wisdom bears eight simultaneous and successive nourishing crops.

In all of us, those fruits are in various stages of maturity. Some of us are only exhibiting little buds of peace; others have maturing, nearly ripe peace. The Lord of the Harvest is working in our lives to bring all of these fruits to robust achievement. He does this by fertilizing us with the fellowship of other believers, by shining on us with His presence, by showering us with the Word, and by pruning us back through discipline.

As peacemakers, let us cultivate this fruit. May we watch for its growth in our lives.

Here is a list of characteristics of wise fruits of peace:

- *God's wisdom does not corrupt the hearer.* God gives it carefully to people whose hearts are ready to accept it and be purified by it. The wisdom of God has the same effect on us as homemade lye soap has on dirty-mouthed kids: It leaves us chastened, purified, and ready for peace!

- *The pure, peaceable wisdom of God does not foster spiritual pride.* God does not want us to lord ourselves over sinners or those less mature in the Lord. If we do, this only points out our own unworthiness in the face of God's grace.

- *God's pure, peaceable wisdom does not stimulate self-sufficiency.* Instead, it produces poverty of spirit, as we realize our desperate need for God and the gifts He gives us through one another.

- *The peaceable wisdom from God does not hand you a loaded gun of snappy repartee and wit to destroy others.* Instead, it gives you insight to bring about supernatural healing and help. It whispers encouragement to failure, applies the holy balm of tranquility to the distraught, pours the oil of healing over the wounded, works reconciliation between hostile parties, and brings reprieve for the condemned.

- *Considerate, peaceable wisdom—God's wisdom—brings, as Matthew Arnold said, "sweet reasonableness."*

- *Considerate, peaceable wisdom of God dictates that although we are aware of the sordid details in any given situation, we still act with compassion, not condemnation.* This does not mean weakness; it means clemency—if clemency will help the condemned.

- *Considerate, peaceable wisdom fully understands the complexities and crudities of a situation, but also knows what solution to apply.* It can discern the difference between punishment and discipline.

- *Wise, peaceable submission from God understands that responsibility and cooperation foster peace.* The King James Version phrases submission as "easy to be entreated"; this doesn't carry the same baggage the word "submission" does today. But whatever words we use, wise submission brings about a bumper crop of peace. Submission doesn't mean being inferior, nor does easy to be entreated mean being weak and gullible. Instead, both mean coming together and cooperating for the purpose of building the Kingdom.

True peaceable wisdom is not rigid and uncompromising about the nonessential rituals of the faith. Rather, those who are easy to be entreated are approachable. They don't think all truth and light begin and end with them. They listen and wisely yield to the moving of the Holy Spirit—even when it is through someone else's initiative. If the pastor and members of every church in the world heard this truth, surely it would end all the wrangling and permit us to turn our attention to those who need to hear the Good News.

- *Wise, peaceable mercy—God's mercy—understands and applies pity that brings peace with it.* Most of us feel bad for someone who is unjustly suffering; not all of us have pity on someone who brought his troubles upon himself—and yet God pitied us even when we were in the midst of our selfishness and confusion. He loved us when we were yet sinners; His love sought us and offered us amnesty when we were separated from Him. When we are wise and seeking peace with mercy, we don't look for revenge; we look for reconciliation. Heavenly mercy is not merely an emotion; it seeks peace by acting on forgiveness.

- *Wise, peaceable, good fruit from God's wisdom produces the fruit of the Spirit, including peace.* A bounty of healthy qualities is cultivated in the life of the person who yields to the Holy Spirit. Those are love, joy, peace, patience, kindness, goodness, faithfulness, gentleness, and self-control. (Galatians 5:22)

- *Wise, peaceable impartiality from God's wisdom does not show favoritism.* Those filled with the Holy Spirit are not status-seeking, keep-up-with-the-Joneses-type people. They know what God values, and that sets the standard for their own assessments. When meeting individuals, they do not ask themselves, "Can this person help me gain wealth or influence?" and then gauge their response to the person upon the answer. Rather, they ask, "Does

God value this person?" and upon the basis of that answer, they set the worth of the person.

- *Wise, peaceable sincerity from God's wisdom is not hypocritical.* For peacemakers, religion is not an act for Sunday morning; it is an honest, daily-lived faith.

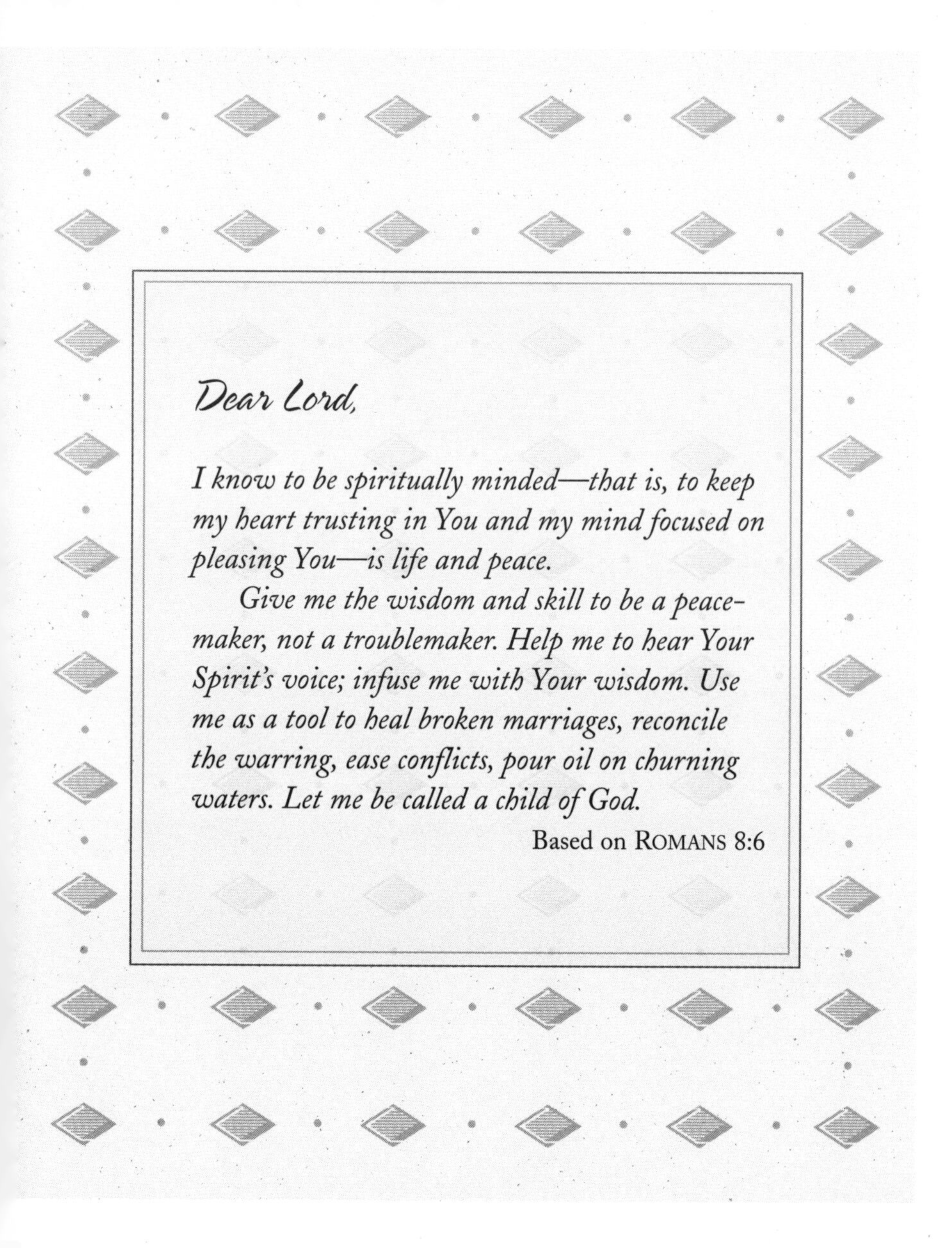

Dear Lord,

I know to be spiritually minded—that is, to keep my heart trusting in You and my mind focused on pleasing You—is life and peace.

Give me the wisdom and skill to be a peacemaker, not a troublemaker. Help me to hear Your Spirit's voice; infuse me with Your wisdom. Use me as a tool to heal broken marriages, reconcile the warring, ease conflicts, pour oil on churning waters. Let me be called a child of God.

Based on ROMANS 8:6

Chapter 7

Peace with Others

If it be possible, as much as lieth in you, live peaceably with all men.
ROMANS 12:18

The beginnings of strife should be avoided. Never expect offenses and if they come, do not recognize them, is a good and safe rule. If they are forced upon you, forgive them as soon as possible. Having forgiven, speedily forget. One cannot put memory to a worse use than to make it the repository of resentment. Whoever declares, "I can forgive, but I cannot forget," has not been taught by the school of Christ.
MARGARET E. SANGSTER

*"Whoever would love life
and see good days must keep
his tongue from evil and
his lips from deceitful speech.
He must turn from evil and do good;
he must seek peace and pursue it.
For the eyes of the Lord are
on the righteous and his ears are
attentive to their prayer,
but the face of the Lord
is against those who do evil."*

1 PETER 3:10–12 NIV

The Three Monkeys

Speak No Evil

Whoever it is, whether your boss, your in-laws, or the garbage man, DO NOT bad-mouth anyone. Oftentimes, this is very, very hard; after all, some people make themselves huge targets for criticism because of their peculiarities, peccadilloes, and problems. No matter. Don't be the one who throws the darts. You may make your criticism in confidence, thinking, *This person will not tell anyone that I said this*—but you have no way of knowing that, and you could inflict great harm and offense upon someone.

If you want to live in peace with others, keep evil, unkind, unflattering comments to yourself. Never say anything about anyone that you would be unwilling to say directly to that person's face. If you must discuss someone, talk it over with the Lord when you pray for him or her.

Hear No Evil

Be the dead-letter office when it comes to gossip. Just don't pass it on. If you want to live in peace with other people, consider gossipy tidbits to be like lice: Don't share them; do them in.

See No Evil

Pursue peace by not being easily offended. Some people are as touchy as cactus in their relationships with other people. They look for reasons to be upset by the actions of others.

If you want to live in peace with others, be slow to assume that a slight was directed at you or that insult was intended. Even then, be slow to take offense.

The Peace Sown in Apology

Apologize when you're wrong. If you've wronged someone, step up to the plate and admit your failing. Don't let pride keep you from saying "I'm sorry." Those words may not wipe away all the pain you caused, but they can go a long way toward healing the harm.

A stockbroker friend said that a fellow male employee behaved in a very bad manner toward his female supervisor. He didn't like her, didn't think she was competent, didn't think she understood the business, and didn't like being under the management of a woman. He took every opportunity to try to publicly embarrass her. He succeeded so well that rumor had it he was about to be fired!

After a particularly bad scene in a meeting, my friend pulled him aside. "You're going to have to quit that and apologize or you're going to be fired," he told the man.

The man was immediately sobered by this news. He didn't want to lose his job—but apologize? "I can't apologize," he told my friend. "I can't tell that woman that I'm sorry."

"You'd better," my friend informed him, "or you're going to be packing a cardboard box with your personal effects before the day is out."

Reluctantly, mostly in the interest of keeping his job, the man went to his female supervisor and humbly apologized. To his great surprise, she began to cry. She outlined a sketchy picture of the tremendous pressures and responsibilities she was facing both on the job and at home. The man was stunned that she was able to do as well as she was under the circumstances. After his meeting, he sent her a bouquet of flowers just to cheer her up. This time, he sincerely wanted to apologize again for the trouble he caused.

By the way, he did keep his job.

If you want to live in peace with people, admit when you are wrong, apologize, and correct your behavior.

I exhort therefore, that, first of all, supplications, prayers, intercessions, and giving of thanks, be made for all men; For kings, and for all that are in authority; that we may lead a quiet and peaceable life in all godliness and honesty. For this is good and acceptable in the sight of God our Savior.

1 TIMOTHY 2:1–3

The Dream Garden of Peace
What If Christians Prayed?

- What would happen if all of the Christians in your place of work prayed that their employer would be prudent and fair-minded?

- What would happen in our churches if all Christian believers would pray for their pastors? What would happen if instead of criticizing the sermon, they prayed that he would have inspiration? What would happen if instead of complaining that he wasn't doing the job, they prayed that the pastor would see the church's needs and that God would bestow the spiritual gifts to meet them?

- What would happen in our towns if all Christian believers who lived there would pray for their mayor? If they prayed that he or she would understand the community? If they prayed that he or she would bring jobs, prosperity, and integrity to the town?

- What would happen to our courts if all Christian believers prayed that justice and mercy would prevail?

- What would happen to our schools if all Christian believers prayed for the superintendents, principals, and teachers?

- What would happen in our state government if all Christian believers who lived there prayed that their governors would be truthful, hardworking, and competent? That their senators would be wise, honorable, and efficient?

- What would happen in our country if all Christian believers would pray for congress, the president, and the supreme court, that they would trust God, that they would be ethical, sagacious, and courageous?

What would happen? Peace.

David: One Whose Life Grew the Rare Fruit of God's Peace

Seek peace, and pursue it. PSALM 34:14

Strange words to be penned by a man of war such as David, but none understand the treasure of peace like those who have been embattled. As the rest of this psalm points out, David experienced God's peace in the midst of life's skirmishes because peace, rather than conquest, was his goal.

The lions may grow weak and hungry, but those who seek the LORD lack no good thing. PSALM 34:10 NIV

As a mere boy with the welfare of his father's flocks upon his shoulders, David understood the value of a quiet, peaceful day and night; he had faced hungry lions and bears that sought to kill him so they could plunder the sheep. David's point in this verse: Even the powerful will pass away, but God provides for His peace-seeking children.

The angel of the LORD encamps around those who fear him, and he delivers them. PSALM 34:7 NIV

As a youth David was armed with only a sling and five rocks when he faced a giant. But he knew that confidence and peace of mind came from treating God with respect. God fought for David even when he confronted a giant foe.

A righteous man may have many troubles, but the LORD *delivers him from them all.* PSALM 34:19 NIV

As a young man whose father-in-law, the king, was actively seeking to kill him, David understood the peaceful refuge the Lord offers. He was shielded from his enemy because his heart was right with God.

The LORD *redeems his servants; no one will be condemned who takes refuge in him.* PSALM 34:22 NIV

As an outcast from his country, David understood the sanctuary of God's provision. He received succor from the people of the land when he was all alone. Like David, seek to serve the Lord; let Him take care of you. If you do, you will find a place of safety in Him.

Evil will slay the wicked; the foes of the righteous will be condemned. PSALM 34:21 NIV

As a king whose land was coveted by his neighbors, David knew the value of having the Lord fighting with him. He achieved victory over his enemies again and again.

The LORD is close to the brokenhearted and saves those who are crushed in spirit. PSALM 34:18 NIV

As a man whose own son stirred up rebellion against him, David grasped the value of a peaceful, harmonious family. Although God sent him a remarkable and wise son named Solomon, his relationship with God still gave him the most peace and comfort.

Do not repay anyone evil for evil. . . . If it is possible, as far as it depends on you, live at peace with everyone. Do not take revenge, my friends, but leave room for God's wrath, for it is written: "It is mine to avenge; I will repay," says the Lord. On the contrary: "If your enemy is hungry, feed him; if he is thirsty, give him something to drink. In doing this, you will heap burning coals on his head." Do not be overcome by evil, but overcome evil with good. ROMANS 12:17–20 NIV

Karen struggled with Paul's concept, "If it is possible. . .live at peace with everyone."

"I wanted to live at peace with my husband, but we had problems of great magnitude between us," said Karen. "He was really good to three of our four children, but it seemed like he hated one of them. This child could not do anything right!

"My husband would say awful things to him, horrible things no person should ever utter to another, especially not to a child! He sometimes physically attacked him, too, for no reason. On numerous occasions, I had to place myself between my husband and this child to protect him."

For many years, Karen kept this family secret to herself, but the violence and terror only escalated. "I believe that a wife should respect her husband and not undermine his authority as the head of the household, but my husband was being sadistically cruel to this child and he refused to see it."

Karen spent many hours on her knees before God seeking guidance for this situation. "The Lord finally opened up my eyes to some principles from the Scriptures. First of all, when Sapphira went along with her husband Ananias's plot to lie, God struck her dead, too (Acts 5). Her obedience belonged to God first and her husband second. If her husband wanted her to be a party to something that was wrong, she should not have done it. I realize that concept might seem obvious to some people, but it was a revelation to me.

"Secondly, the Lord showed me the Scripture that said if anyone causes a little child to stumble, it would be better if that person had a millstone tied around his neck and were cast into the sea. My husband's behavior was affecting our child in numerous ways, including spiritually.

"Also, I discovered verses that said if I confronted my husband with his fault and he refused to listen to me, I should get a godly person in the church to talk to him about his behavior. If he refused to listen to that person, then I should get more Christian people to confront his behavior and pray for him. And then, if he still wouldn't listen, I should pray for him as if he weren't a Christian believer at all."

Karen and other Christian believers prayerfully confronted her husband on several occasions. Her husband denied he was abusive to the child—but his behavior slowly changed toward his son. "He knew other people were aware of his behavior," Karen said, "even though he denied he had a problem. But abuse can only succeed in secret. Once an abusive person knows that others are on to him, he eventually has to face up to himself, and I know the prayers helped!

"If it has to go that far, confronting in love with the goal of restoration is a powerful tool. The person may shout down one person, but it is hard for him to say that everyone is wrong. It gives you a better chance of working out the problem. Through prayer and His Word, God helped me to know how to approach the situation, handle it effectively, and live in peace with my husband and my family."

Godly Principles for Restoring Peace in Relationships

Be a peacemaker, but not gutless. If you are a peace-loving person who hates confrontation, you may not easily challenge problems head-on. You may be the sort of person who prefers to tolerate problems and adjust. Sometimes, that is the wisest course. As Solomon wrote: "A wrathful man stirreth up strife: but he that is slow to anger appeaseth strife" (Proverbs 15:18). With a serious, damaging problem, however, appeasement is not the path to peacemaking. It may even prolong the problem rather than rectify it. If the problem is serious, chances are it won't go away; it may go underground only to surface later and cause further destruction.

Paul's teaching on the subject was succinct and to the point: "Let us therefore make every effort to do what leads to peace and to mutual edification" (Romans 14:19 NIV). In other words, choose your battles carefully. Make sure you are confronting an issue of importance rather than making a big deal out of a minor irritation.

Approach the problem on your knees. If you can—although sometimes you can't because of a sudden eruption of conflict—spend some time asking God for guidance, wisdom, forgiveness, and grace for yourself, and an open, willing heart for the other person.

Even if the Holy Spirit doesn't urge you to confront the people with their flaws, pray that their eyes will be opened to see truly. If you recognize a flaw in someone, you are responsible to pray that that person will see the truth and repent.

Confront in love, not anger. This is especially true if you have a bad temper! A hot temper and a big mouth may cause you to say things that drive an even deeper wedge between you and the person whom you need to confront. Wait until you cool off, and there is not so much emotion flowing.

Keep in mind your main goal. You want to show the other person the fault that is damaging his or her own life, your life, the lives of others, the person's relationship with God, or even other people's relationships with God. You want to show the wrongs so you can heal, not kill.

Don't attack the person; attack the flaw. To berate a person for being a bad person is a little like one leper scolding another leper for being ill. We all have faults and are flawed. That's a given. Your job as peacemaker is to point out how one particular flaw is damaging to the person and others.

In other words, to say, "You lied to me on Friday night when you said. . ." is by far preferable to "You are a liar!" The fact that the person is a liar is a given because as sinners, we are all liars. Deal with the action. To charge the person with being a liar is not your responsibility because that would make you judge of another person, something the Scriptures strictly warn against. Judging the person is the job of God and Him alone. We are, however, allowed to be "fruit inspectors" because, as Jesus said, "By their fruit you will know them." Deal with what the person has done. Let the Holy Spirit deal with who the person is.

Be specific. Blanket indictments are uncalled for and unhelpful. Tell the person exactly what behavior to which you object. None of this, "You always leave the bathroom in a big mess!" Rather, "Today, you left your towel and dirty clothing on the floor, whiskers in the sink, shaving soap on the cabinet knobs, and water splatters on the mirror. It made a lot of extra work for me."

Ask for an apology or restoration. If the person doesn't know what you want, he or she may not know how to respond. But since your goal is to restore the person and strengthen the relationship, you must tell the person what to do if he or she doesn't know.

Zacchaeus, the tax collector, knew exactly what to do when he met Jesus and repented of his sins. "Look, Lord," he said spontaneously, "if I have cheated anybody out of anything, I will pay back four times the amount!" (Luke 19:8 NIV) Other people, however, may need a little prodding or a suggestion or two to figure out how to restore the relationship. But if they are truly sorry, they will want to restore. They will want to ask forgiveness even if they find the words themselves hard to say.

Be ready to forgive—and forget. Some people find this hardest of all, but it is so necessary! Remember: If you don't forgive, God can't forgive you. If you need help forgiving, appeal to the throne of God. He understands forgiveness.

Consider your own mistakes and be humble. Don't get all puffed up because you have seen someone's flaws and have been called to confront him or her. All of us are in danger of sin—and one of these is spiritual pride!

The Salty Seeds of Grace and Peace

Everyone will be salted with fire. "Salt is good, but if it loses its saltiness, how can you make it salty again? Have salt in yourselves, and be at peace with each other."

MARK 9:49–50 NIV

With acrid smoke and incense curling around his head, the priest stood before the temple altar, sacrifice in hand. Before he put the meat on the coals, he salted it—not to purify it but to season it because it was food for God's use. "May this sacrifice be pleasing to the LORD," was the prayer of the worshiper, "and may I be pleasing to Him, too."

The sheep, goats, and doves are no longer slaughtered, salted, and laid on the fire for our sin. The perfect sacrifice of Jesus put an end to the bloodshed once and for all time. In emulation of Christ, we offer ourselves to God as "living sacrifices," seasoned with grace to make us acceptable to God and laid upon His altar.

Give a little grace. Extend it to those around you. Make peace in Jesus' name by giving grace.

Jesus commanded us to make peace with others in a parable about a man who owed his king a tremendous sum of money. When the debt came due, he could not pay it, so the debtor begged for more time. The king didn't extend the repayment; he canceled the loan!

The man, having dodged debtors' prison and slavery, found a fellow servant of the king who owed him a pittance and demanded repayment. When the fellow servant asked for an extension, he refused and threw him into prison.

At the end of the story, the king rescinded his forgiveness and had the first man thrown into prison until he could pay all he owed. Jesus ended His story by concluding, "This is how my heavenly Father will treat each of you unless you forgive your brother from your heart" (Matthew 18:35 NIV).

You have been given grace; give grace. You have been forgiven; forgive. You have been given the Prince of Peace; give peace.

In my distress I cried unto the LORD and he heard me. Deliver my soul, O LORD, from lying lips, and from a deceitful tongue. . . . My soul hath long dwelt with him that hateth peace. I am for peace: but when I speak, they are for war.

PSALM 120:1–2, 6–7

Sowing the Seeds of Peace with the Warlike

Does this sound like the situation in your office? Your school? Your home? Your church? You want to get along with everyone, cooperate, live at peace, get something accomplished, but you are the only one who does! Everyone else likes to keep the conflict going.

No matter how great a Christian you are, how well intended you are, you may not be able to bring everyone together to sing "Kum Ba Ya" and be nice to one another. But you can claim the peace of Christ for yourself in the midst of the storm.

Blooming in the Battle

Hillary's job in the high-pressure world of newspaper reporting was made even more stressful by the situation in the newsroom.

"I came in to a really bad situation," said Hillary. She was hired to work the desk of a highly regarded reporter who had been fired by the publisher for slanting the news against "Henry Jones," a highly placed public official. Hillary was aware the publisher was on one side of the issue while all the newsroom opposed him. A large public constituency supported each side, and the community was increasingly polarized over the issues and the man. Hillary didn't know what the truth was about Jones, but she resolved to be fair—wherever it led.

"I tend to be easygoing, and I try hard to be fair and honest, but I knew eventually somebody was going to be out to get me; I just didn't know which faction, the publisher or the newsroom. It was a touchy situation, but I believed the Lord and I could handle it. I prayed for wisdom every time I filed a story," said Hillary.

Hillary found her coworkers friendly but cautious and snoopy. "As I started getting into touch with Jones and other public officials, they listened in on my phone conversations to see which way I was leaning. They would access my personal computer files through the network. They never came right out and asked me, 'Are you for us or with the publisher? Are you for Jones or against him?' but they questioned me closely to find out what I was thinking.

"You see, early in the 1900s, a reporter just related the facts and let the reader make up his mind. But the philosophy from the 1950s until the present is that a reporter is supposed to tell the reader what to think. I don't agree with that. I believe John Q. Public should make up his own mind on any given issue. I may have strong feelings on any given subject, but I'm not going to impose that on the readers.

"I especially felt that way about Jones. I would report what

Jones said and what he did, but I refused to put any slant on it. When people privately asked me for my opinion, I would decline to give it, and that made both sides angry—especially the anti-Jones faction. No one knew it, but I strongly suspected that Jones was involved in a lot of dirty business, but I didn't have the proof. I wasn't going to hang the man on suspicion. I would let him build his own gallows, tie the rope around his own neck—and then I'd report on the hanging."

Over time, death threats came from the anti-Jones faction. "I was in the schizophrenic position of being threatened by the faction I agreed with and comforted by the faction I suspected! I prayed long and hard about the situation. I don't like to cause trouble, but I won't run scared, either," she said.

Hillary felt that the Spirit directed her to take a small tape recorder to all of her interviews with Jones. She didn't know exactly why, but she obeyed, and very shortly, she was glad she had.

Soon after, Hillary filed a story about Jones and left for the day. When she returned, she discovered that the newsroom had slanted the story to say things against Jones that weren't true. "I thought, *If they're going to throw mud at Jones, at least throw it for the true reasons!* I gave the tape to the publisher. He listened to it and agreed that the story the newsroom ran was slanted to the point of inaccuracy. He reran the story with a heading explaining that the reporter (me) had filed an accurate story, but that the newsroom had slanted it. He then fired the editor!"

The situation continued to swirl with even the FBI becoming involved because of Jones's suspected mishandling of public funds. "Over time, Jones has, in fact, hung himself," said Hillary. "I've never publicly commented either way, but I got a very accurate story.

"What the Lord has taught me is that I am called to be His light in this newsroom, in my home, and in my community. If I ask God to glorify Himself in me, I don't have to worry about the outcome. I can trust Him in the storm."

And I will give peace in the land,
and ye shall lie down,
and none shall make you afraid:
and I will rid evil beasts
out of the land,
neither shall the sword
go through your land.

LEVITICUS 26:6

Better is little with the fear of the LORD than great treasure and trouble therewith. Better is a dinner of herbs where love is, than a stalled ox and hatred therewith.

PROVERBS 15:16–17

Better is a dry morsel, and quietness therewith, than an house full of sacrifices with strife.

PROVERBS 17:1

Dear Lord,

You have been made our peace. I know that when my ways please You, You make even my enemies to be at peace with me. Help me to refrain my tongue from evil and my lips that they speak no deceit. Remind me to pray rather than criticize, encourage instead of complain, and be part of the solution instead of the problem.

Based on MATTHEW 5:9
PROVERBS 16:7; 1 PETER 3:10

Chapter 8

A Harvest of Family Peace

Behold,
how good and how pleasant
it is for brethren to
dwell together in unity!

PSALM 133:1

Family unity is everyone's dream. It certainly was God's dream when He established the family. But unfortunately, the painful reality is that the opposite is often true. In Psalm 6, David certainly knew whereof he was speaking, having had the opposite experience. In any given family, everybody knows the pecking order, and David certainly knew his: He was considered "least likely to succeed" among his brothers. If he had any doubts about that, a visit from the prophet Samuel cemented this in his mind!

When Samuel came to Bethlehem to anoint a new king for Israel from the sons of Jesse, he invited Jesse and his sons to a sacrifice to God and planned to announce the new king of Israel at that time. Jesse was aware of Samuel's intentions, and brought seven of his eight sons to the sacrifice. David, the youngest, was assigned the sheep-keeping duties for the day because, after all, no one even considered David a contender! Samuel had to ask repeatedly, "Are these all of your sons?" until as an afterthought, Jesse said reluctantly, "Well, there is one more!" and sent for David.

Of course, Samuel anointed David as the future king of Israel. Even that didn't give David much status with the folks at home, though. When war broke out between Israel and the Philistines, the three older brothers declared their allegiance to Saul and went off to the battle with him. David, the newly anointed king, was again left at home to take care of the sheep.

On an errand to take provisions to the camp, David overheard the Philistine giant Goliath's challenge to send one Israelite to fight him man-to-man. When David indignantly asked, "Who is this Philistine to challenge the armies of the Most High?" he incurred the wrath of his brother Eliab, who in so many words demanded, "Just who do you think you are, you conceited little pip-squeak? Did you just come down here to cause trouble? I know what an evil heart you have!"

As translated, David's exact words were: "Now what have I done? Can't I even speak?" Sound familiar?

The Bible does give rules for family unity—if only everyone would cooperate and live by them! So how do we put biblical principles into practice so our homes are havens of peace?

Tips for Planting Family Peace

Don't permit negative names to be used. The Bible emphasizes the important connection between names and self-image from the beginning of the Book to the end. God changed Abram (meaning "father") to Abraham (meaning "father of the multitude") when He gave him the promise of a son with Sarah. In the Book of Revelation, the overcomers are presented a white stone with a new name on it, one given to them by God.

To allow children or adults to taunt—even "in fun"—can cause lasting harm. Teasing nicknames can be destructive, causing hurt feelings that eventually produce discord in the family. Appellations such as stupid, dummy, idiot, moron, and so on, should never be allowed. Encourage the use of affectionate, kind, uplifting words as pet names.

Curb jealousies by not making comparisons or choosing favorite children. Never, never, never begin a sentence with, "When your brother was your age, he. . ." and then complete the sentence with some wonderful feat accomplished by the sibling. Comparisons are fine when the child is on equal footing with his brother, such as, "When your brother was your age, he had lots of growing pains, too." Or, "When your brother was your age, he had trouble with his complexion, too." But never, "When your brother was your age, he could leap tall buildings with a single bound!"

Making comparisons and choosing a favorite child was the undoing of Jacob's family. Jacob honored Joseph as his favorite child, made this evident to his other sons, and permitted Joseph to taunt them as well. Jacob, as the father and perpetrator of the unfairness, and Joseph who behaved badly toward his brothers, suffered greatly as the result (Genesis 37).

Each child is a unique, special gift from God and should be regarded as such.

Don't provoke your children—or any other family member—to anger (Ephesians 6:4, Colossians 3:21). Some parents are the cause of the conflict in their families. They consider their actions to be discipline, but instead, they are merely picking at the child. Eventually, the child will give up trying to please you. Don't yell; show the child what you want him to do.

One man said about his large family, "If someone yelled at you in my family when we were growing up, you got out of the house because it was on fire! We had lots of discussions, lots of differing opinions, and it was okay to disagree—but no matter what, we couldn't yell at one another. Mother and Dad would not permit that. You lost your right to speak if you yelled."

Have some fun together. Sometimes this is hard because each family seems to have one designated party pooper—occasionally more. However, don't let this keep you from having fun as a family. But make the rules clear: We're going to do such and such. It will be a fun family time. All will attend in a pleasant mood and cooperate with one another with good attitudes. If you cannot do this, say so up front, and we'll have fun without you. If one person is persistent in spoiling everyone's fun, as hard as it sounds, you may have to excuse him or her from that activity. Don't allow one person to ruin family unity for everyone.

After a tragedy, families especially need to enjoy themselves together. Despite what you may hear, nothing can tear a family apart like catastrophe and the resulting tensions and high emotions. However, if you can put some fun between your family and the calamity, it helps to give you all perspective and respite while at the same time it unifies you. "Fun" can be something as simple and inexpensive as a walk in the park, but it needs to special and pleasurable.

Recall your blessings. On several occasions, Moses reminded the people to tell their children what God had done for them (Exodus 10:2, 12:26, 27). Reminisce about the difficulties your family has faced together and how God has brought you through. This builds unity and peace within the family.

Set aside times to recall your family's blessings as opportunities to praise God. At the dinner table before saying grace, make a family tradition in which each member gives a short word of thanksgiving for something God has done that day.

So You Think You Have Problems. . .
While many families are in conflict and crisis today, our problems are really not so different than they were in Bible times because people are people, and we make the same mistakes as our forefathers. As with every issue of life, the Bible speaks clearly about family problems and demonstrates how to bring peace and resolution. Take a look at some of these Bible families, their problems, and solutions—good and bad. You may find that your family's difficulties are not so unique after all!

- *Disobedience, rebellion, and reconciliation*—God, the perfect Father, created a perfect environment in a perfect world and placed in it two perfect people, but the people still got all messed up anyway! God punished them by making them leave the Garden of Eden and work for their food, but reconciled all His children to Himself with the most sacrificial example of love—the death of His beloved Son.

- *Violent sibling jealousy and loving acceptance*—Here was a terrible situation for the first family to face! Cain, the elder, was jealous of God's blessing on his younger brother, Abel. So in a fit of rage, Cain killed

Abel. When confronted by God, Cain denied his culpability—"Am I my brother's keeper?"—adding rebellion to his load of guilt. God's answer to Abel's question was, "Yes, you are your brother's keeper and you are responsible for your own actions, too." Because Cain showed no remorse, God banished him from the family, but at Cain's request, still showed compassion on him and extended His protection over this wayward boy.

- *Drunken, embarrassing family member and protection*—After the epic flood, Noah parked the ark and returned to his first occupation—farming. From his vineyard, he made some wine and proceeded to get drunk, a despicable act in that, or any, culture. His son Ham spotted his inebriated father passed out and naked inside the tent. Ham mockingly told his brothers. The other two boys covered their father's nakedness to prevent him any further embarrassment. God punished Ham for his disrespect.

- *Conflict over property*—Both Abraham and his nephew Lot were successful shepherds, and when conflict arose concerning pastureland, Abraham gave Lot first choice as to which fields he wanted. Lot greedily chose the best for himself. God prospered Abraham anyway. Lot's fields, flocks, home, and wife were destroyed with Sodom and Gomorrah.

- *Rivalry between stepbrothers*—Both sons of Abraham but by two different mothers, Ishmael taunted and teased his younger brother Isaac. The conflict spread to the two mothers. Abraham separated the two women and their sons, which proved a temporary solution. This particular family feud continues to this day between the descendants of Ishmael, or the Arabs, and the descendants of Isaac, or the Jews.

- *Finding an appropriate mate*—When Isaac needed a wife, Abraham painstakingly arranged a marriage for him, not with any of the local heathen girls, but with Rebekah who was of the same culture, religion, and practices as Isaac. This proved to be a loving, successful marriage.

- *Parental favoritism*—The twin sons of Isaac and Rebekah, Esau and Jacob, were of very different natures. Isaac preferred Esau; Rebekah favored Jacob. Rebekah conspired with Jacob to steal an important parental blessing from Esau. Jacob had to run for his life. For a time, the brothers were estranged, but they eventually made peace with one another.

- *A child born at an inconvenient time*—Moses' parents already had two children when an Egyptian pharaoh decreed that only female children should be allowed to live. When Moses was born, they kept him hidden as long as possible. Moses' mother hid him in the river where he was discovered and adopted by a royal princess. Eventually, Moses was restored to the family.

- *In-law problems*—Aaron and Miriam, Moses' brother and sister, did not like their brother's choice of wife primarily because of her race. Moses stood by his choice and God sent a plague on Miriam until they both apologized.

- *A foolish mate*—When David was operating a covert army in the desert, he asked Nabal for provisions. Nabal—a name which literally means "fool"—refused although David had protected his interests. Angry, David planned to wipe out Nabal's entire holdings. Upon hearing of this, Abigail, Nabal's wife, gave David's army provisions, and her husband and family were spared.

- *Undisciplined children*—Israel's high priest Eli had two sons who were cheating God with Eli's full knowledge but disapproval. In ignoring the situation, Eli brought the judgment of God down upon his entire house.

- *Unnatural affection between siblings*—David's son Ammon fell in love with his beautiful half-sister, Tamir. He planned a seduction which turned into a rape. David did not deal with his son's sin and caused a family feud.

Peace with a Purpose

There are golden moments to teach peace in the life of a family and individual. Because it takes conflict to teach peaceful resolution, the best lessons often revolve around childhood infractions of the rules of the house. A little sense of humor helps, as illustrated in this story written by an elderly man.

"In the 1920s, my parents had a nice-sized farm in northern Illinois. Every year, we had neighboring threshers come to harvest the wheat crop. It was during one these times that Mother and Dad taught me a valuable lesson about family cooperation.

"My mother had sent me to fill the wood box for what seemed like the one-hundredth time that day. Mother was cooking for the threshers, and she was very testy. Fuming, I trudged out to the woodshed and loaded up an armful of wood. It was then that I found a mouse nest.

"The mother mouse, nursing her young, looked at me in astonishment, then scampered off. Her five pink hairless babies squeaked in protest. In spite of the fact that they were very cute, I knew my duty was to dispatch them to their reward. I was about to call a kitty to act as executioner when an idea crossed my mind. I scooped up the babies and put them in my shirt pocket. I had just enough time to implement my plan.

"My mother was known far and wide as a superb cook and housekeeper. She kept her kitchen immaculate—no easy task on a busy farm—and her reputation for cleanliness was a point of pride to her. Even though our house was always cleaned near the point of sterilization, the coming of the threshers sent Mother into a positive scouring frenzy. She knew that the neighboring housewives would closely question their menfolk on the tastiness and abundance of the meal and the state of orderliness of the house, and if Mother expected to maintain her reputation as patron saint of the Order of Lye Soap, everything would have to be perfect. Being a rebellious boy who was angry about being on wood box detail instead of out with the men and machines in the field, my sinful little mind hatched a plot that was revenge masquerading as a joke.

"Wood box filled, Mother proceeded to order me around in her best drill sergeant manner. 'Scour those sawhorses!' 'More water in the teakettle!' 'Set the table!' 'More wood!' Amid these commands, I found opportunity—as well as motivation—to put the five little mice on the bean salad.

"Mother's bean salad was another of her specialties. She made it with chopped boiled eggs, pickles, salad dressing, bacon, chickpeas, and about four different kinds of beans. I thought the tiny mice looked like chickpeas with arms and legs. I thought the threshers would see them, think it was a big joke, tease Mother, discard the mice, and the meal would go on as usual—except that I'd have gotten revenge on Mother for ordering me around. Obviously, there were a few factors I had not taken into consideration.

"After the dinner bell rang and the men washed up under the trees, the meal began with Dad returning thanks. As I watched the sun-beaten faces of the men become reverent during the prayer, I relished the thought of the joke I was playing on them—and Mother. "Amen," Dad said, and all the men echoed it. Then began the parade of food from the kitchen. Platters of fried chicken and roast beef, bowls of gravy, mashed potatoes, green beans with onion and bacon, fresh peas, candied carrots, hot bread, and macaroni salad made their way up and down the table. Mother sent me to the springhouse for more butter, and when I returned, the bean salad was already halfway around the table. I was puzzled as to why I had heard no hue and cry about the mice. Then to my horror, I realized that the little creatures were awaiting their doom under the beans on someone's plate. I only wanted to play a joke on Mother: I didn't really want my neighbors to eat baby mice!

"The meal finished without incident. The men napped briefly under the trees while we cleaned up the table and snacked on leftovers. To my surprise, Mother even agreed to let me go to the field for the afternoon.

"I sort of forgot about the mice. I was bone-tired from the day and ready to climb into my bed when, upon pulling back the sheets, I found what had become of them. Startled, I yelped. The little mice lay in eternal repose upon my pillow! 'I could have put them in your breakfast oatmeal,' Mother said. She and Dad stood in the doorway.

" 'I want to take care of another pest in the woodshed,' Dad said. *'Now.'*

"I made one more trip to the woodshed that day to have further contact with a stout piece of firewood, giving me one more memory of a thrashing from my childhood.

"Hard as it may be for some to understand in a day when

many equate a spanking with abuse, my parents' sense of humor and strict discipline kept peace in our home. We knew that if we were disrespectful, unkind, foolish, or lazy, we would face their calmly administered correction to the seat of the problem. They didn't yell or threaten—they didn't have to. They acted to protect and maintain family peace."

Family Peace under Siege

Dick and Jeanette's large family of sons had their conflicts over the years, but for the most part, they got along very well together.

"The boys used to wrestle and get into scrapes, but afterward, they were all good buddies," said Dick. "They stuck together."

When the two older boys decided to marry, Jeanette was thrilled to finally have some girls in the family. "I loved my daughters-in-law, and we became close," said Jeanette. "I looked forward to my other sons marrying and bringing home more girls. If I only knew!"

When their fourth son, Jason, fell in love with a young woman in his office and brought her home, they were appalled. "We had taught our boys not to date non-Christians, so when we met Marcy, we hardly knew what to make of her!" said Jeanette. "She was a pretty little girl, but she looked like a hoodlum with very short, tight clothing and wild hair. She swore like a longshoreman, and she made it clear to us that she didn't believe in our 'religion'—and that she and my son were going to move in together whether we liked it or not!"

"Jason just acted like a sheep," said Dick. "He followed her around like he'd lost his senses."

"Every time Dick or I tried to get Jason off alone to talk to him," Jeanette added, "Marcy would barge in. I think she was afraid we'd try to break them up—which, of course, was exactly what we had in mind!"

Shortly after their last visit to the couple, Jeanette and Dick received a shocking phone call: Jason and Marcy had eloped. "We were just crushed!" said Jeanette. "I can't begin to tell you how upset we were! We congratulated them, welcomed Marcy to the family, and offered to hold a shower for them. When they came home for the shower, however, it was pretty awful. Marcy flirted with our other sons and relatives—even with Dick!—and by then, Jason knew he'd made a mistake. We had been praying for them, but now we prayed even harder for their love and commitment to God and each other."

When Jason lost his job, the couple asked if they could move home for a while. Dick and Jeanette had to think long and hard about having Marcy under their roof. "We couldn't afford to rent them a separate house, but I wasn't sure how well it would work to have Marcy here," said Dick. "Jason said she didn't want to work now that they were married and that she went out late at night and slept most of the day. He thought if he could get her away from the bad influences, around some Christian people, she might straighten out.

"Jeanette and I didn't feel like it was right to try to separate them since they were married, but we thought we'd better lay down some ground rules if we were going to allow them to come live with us." The ground rules were simple but clear, and both Jason and Marcy agreed to them. No liquor or cigarettes or drugs in the house. Everybody pitched in and helped with whatever work needed to be done. Everybody went to church on Sunday morning and evening and Wednesday night. The Lord's name was not to be used in vain.

"After they moved in, things were fine for about six hours," said Jeanette. Then the family was caught up in a maelstrom of conflict and fighting. With no place else for them to go, betting that Dick and Jeanette would not throw them out, Marcy pushed the limits of everyone's endurance. "We should have put them on the street the first time Marcy swore," said Dick, "but we kept hoping she'd learn. I guess we were the ones who learned!"

Finally, Jason found a job, saved a little money, and moved

out with Marcy. Their marriage remains rocky, but Jason feels a commitment to try to stay together. Holidays with all of the family together are no longer pleasant, but Dick and Jeanette have hope. "We pray a lot for our boys and their wives. Although they are mostly grown up, we feel a responsibility to lift them up in prayer on a daily basis," said Dick. "I think that's one of our most important jobs as parents. We believe God can change people so we pray that His power falls upon each one of them. Somehow, through everything, we have a sense of peace. We thank God for it. We don't know what the future holds for Jason and Marcy, but we've placed them in God's hands."

The Fragrant Bloom of Peace

Divorces in a small town can be messy but Amelia's had been a particularly bitter, acrimonious one. She had fought it for nearly eight years—seeking professional counseling, praying, begging God to restore her broken home—until she finally put the matter in God's hands and left it there. Her doctor husband, Eric, for his part, continued to carry on a very public affair with his office nurse, while saying all the right words to Amelia and the children. Finally, the whole ridiculous farce ended when the nurse left her husband and children for Eric and demanded that he marry her—or else.

So he did. Now a few months later, Amelia knew she would be facing Eric and his new wife for the first time as a couple at the college graduation party of their oldest son. "I knew this milestone was coming," said Amelia. "It actually took me a year to prepare for it. I would think about it, knowing I would have to face Eric and his girlfriend or new wife, whichever it was going to be, and worry about how I was going to handle it."

Because her son wanted his whole family together for the celebration, Amelia was determined to somehow get through it. "I asked people—my church family and Bible study group—to pray for me," said Amelia, "but when the day dawned, I still didn't feel like I was ready to face my ex-husband and his new wife."

Because her son and two of his friends were all celebrating their graduations, the boys decided to hold a joint party in a nearby town. Amelia's parents wanted her to ride with them, hoping to help support her in the trauma ahead. "I knew if I rode with my parents, my mother would say a lot of negative things about Eric, about how awful it was for me to have to be going through all of this and so forth. But I have an open enough relationship with my parents that I could say, 'You know, I think I need the ride down alone to get my head together.' They accepted that, so I drove alone."

Amelia put on a tape of Christian praise music and worshiped God all the way to the party. By the time she arrived, she recognized God's love wrapped around her; what's more, He had given her a tremendous sense of peace. "I had such a sense of the presence of God and so much peace and tranquility in my spirit," said Amelia. "When I looked at Eric and his new wife, it really was no big deal. There was a little twinge of sadness, but nothing more. Normally, I would have dwelled on how my love was betrayed, how our bright dreams were crushed and tarnished, but instead, I was just very happy for our son's achievement."

The graduation party went so well, and Amelia handled it so easily, that afterward she wondered why she had let it bother her so much. "I was tempted to think, *See! You didn't need God after all! It was no big deal!* But then I realized that if Satan couldn't steal my peace, he would next want to minimize what God had miraculously done for me. 'No,' I said. 'I asked for peace and God gave it!' "

A Prayer for Peace in Families

Dear Lord,

Help me to take heed of myself and diligently keep my soul, never forgetting what You have shown me lest my heart stray. Help me to teach my children the truths You have taught me. Help me to teach them to respect You all of their days.

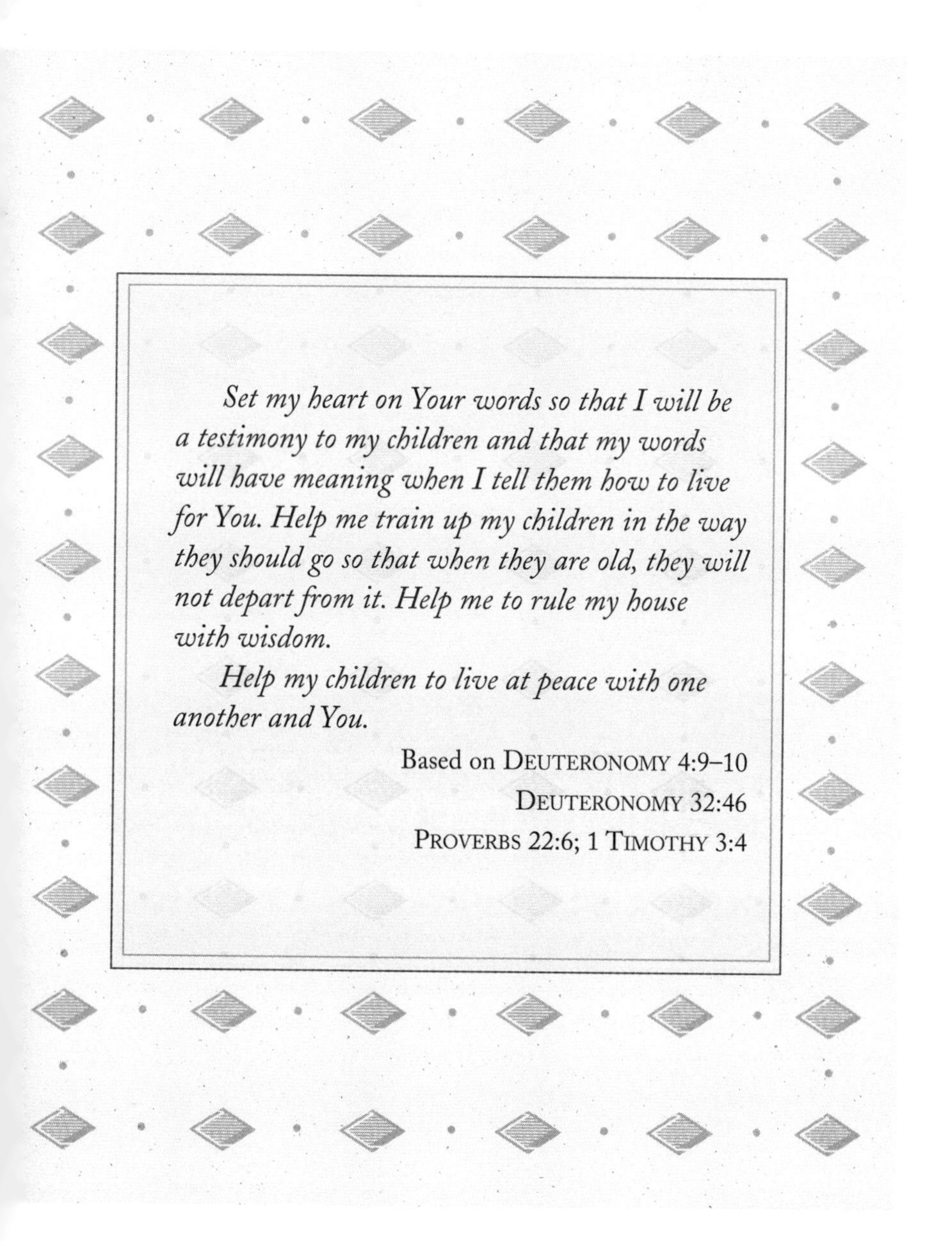

Set my heart on Your words so that I will be a testimony to my children and that my words will have meaning when I tell them how to live for You. Help me train up my children in the way they should go so that when they are old, they will not depart from it. Help me to rule my house with wisdom.

Help my children to live at peace with one another and You.

Based on DEUTERONOMY 4:9–10
DEUTERONOMY 32:46
PROVERBS 22:6; 1 TIMOTHY 3:4

Chapter 9

A Harvest of Peace among God's People:
Seeds of Peace in the Body of Christ

For God is not

the author of confusion,

but of peace,

as in all churches of the saints.

1 CORINTHIANS 14:33

They met in secret, slipping into the house a few at a time under the cover of early dawn. Once, this group of believers met openly at the Jerusalem temple or in a local synagogue, but now, persecution made that dangerous. They convened covertly, just a few believers gathered in private homes but not enough people to attract attention. That way, if someone came in uninvited, they'd just look like a typical family with a distinguished visitor. After all, they were family—the family of God—and they were related by blood—the blood of the Lamb of God.

Today, a former temple prostitute stood along the back wall of the house. She literally "knew" half the men in the room, including the man who was now their teacher. Of course, that was before she and they had all become followers of Christ. Since Jesus purchased her freedom from sin with His blood—and she purchased her freedom from the heathen temple with cold, hard cash—she wove baskets and successfully sold them in the marketplace, making good use of the fair bit she had learned about merchandising over the years.

Beside her stood an impoverished Jewish mother with four small daughters. This house where the believers were meeting was her home; she and her husband were risking their lives and those of their daughters to host their brothers and sisters in Christ. Other than going to the village well and to the market—and from the thin, hungry look of her and the children, that was none too often—this woman barely left her house.

On the other side of the basket weaver was the wife of a Roman general. She, like the Jewish mother, led a cloistered life, but hers was one of great luxury and privilege. Her husband was antagonistic toward Christians, so she came with her identity disguised, and she barely spoke to anyone. She knew the danger she risked, for there were spies in some of the churches. She didn't know who they were, but she knew her husband was bent on stamping out her faith in Jesus, and she didn't want to compromise herself or other fellow believers.

Her personal body servant stood beside her. This Nubian-born slave had introduced her mistress to Christ and had such aptitude for the Word, such anointing from the Holy Spirit, that she was foremost among the women.

This was the composition of the early church, and as a result, the services were sometimes a bit disorganized. Jewish worshipers were accustomed to the solemn synagogue and temple ceremonies that were marked with great debates and heated discussion over weighty manners, where the men attended and participated, but where the women rarely went and never, never took part. The women were now included in the meetings—but some men wondered, *Should all be allowed to attend?*

Meanwhile, the former idolatrous pagans were accustomed to a far more freestyle worship. In their services, provocatively clad male and female priests danced and solicited patronage from the worshipers, while demon-possessed priests fell into screaming, frenzied trances. How were they to worship the true God of heaven? Did the Holy Spirit manifest Himself in tongues the way the demons did through the priests?

Adding to the confusion were the tense, uncertain times; all the believers faced hope, persecution, and the danger of death on every hand. Would Jesus return soon? Or would the chief Jews or Roman soldiers arrest them and confiscate their property and lives before He could return? In the New Testament church, genealogy, rank, and wealth were overwhelmed by the Holy Spirit's anointing. Now slave and master worshiped side by side. Occasionally, a Gentile slave would be a church leader while his Jewish, titled owner served tables.

Each person came to the worship services with something to contribute—a song, a thought, a spiritual message. Sometimes, two or three people brought sermons. Such participation and diversity were both the strength and glory of the church, but they were also an opportunity for disorder. Then, too, people being what they are, competition and bedlam occasionally resulted. Is it any wonder that Paul called for peace in the church?

Churches face some of the same challenges today. Parishioners come from varied backgrounds and different generations. They speak disparate languages, if you will, because the music or style of preaching that appeals and speaks to one group does not always communicate to another. One person feels close to God during a strict liturgical worship; another feels the Spirit move during bluegrass rhythms. Some want to hear hellfire preached; others believe God should be presented as a God of love. Within the same congregation will be people with strong gifts who want to contribute their talents, but they sometimes discover individuals with weaker gifts hold the positions and authority. Gossip, backbiting, and power struggles almost always develop when people are involved together in anything!

Is there any possibility today for peace and unity in the body of Christ? Can the Church ever be made presentable as the bride of Christ, without spots, wrinkles, or blemishes?

In chapter 14 of First Corinthians, the apostle Paul gave instructions for order in the church service, but he prefaced the teaching with another chapter that is the true key to peace. That instruction begins with the following three verses: "If I speak in the tongues of men and of angels, but have not love, I am only a resounding gong or a clanging cymbal. If I have the gift of prophecy and can fathom all mysteries and all knowledge, and if I have a faith that can move mountains, but have not love, I am nothing. If I give all I possess to the poor and surrender my body to the flames, but have not love, I gain nothing" (1 Corinthians 13:1–3 NIV).

This is the key to peace in the body of Christ: self-sacrificing love.

Peace with Those Difficult People

A Barnyard Sonnet of Peace

He was just a tiny thing, about two inches tall, covered with black down and topped with an infinitesimal red comb. The farmer was going to drown him because little Bantam rooster chicks grow up to be big Bantam roosters, all of which transform into ten inches of fuss, feathers, noise, and aggravation. Full grown, there's not enough meat on them to even make a respectable noodle soup, and left to their own devices, they mature into terrible barnyard bullies. They're only good for one thing, and the farmer already had a Bantam rooster for that purpose, so this one was on his way to meeting his Maker.

But because nearly all baby animals are irresistible, and this tiny chick was no exception, we pleaded for his life. The farmer gave him to us with a knowing smile, and we carried him home and presented him to Mother who was supposed to know what to do with all infant creatures.

After twenty-four hours of having a most ungrateful little

chicken as a houseguest, it began to appear that the farmer had the right idea after all. The chick cheeped all the time. He was not happy in his box next to the stove; he didn't want to be held. He was happiest when Mother carried him around in her apron pocket—an arrangement which she considered less than ideal. So when the mother cat had a batch of kittens in a cardboard box on the back porch, we decided to put him in with them. His day-and-night cheeping was getting on everybody's nerves, and we figured she'd either let him cuddle in with her or eat him—either way, he'd be quiet.

Mama cat knew he was different. At first, she was worried about him, but her mother instincts triumphed, and after all, a baby was a baby so she'd take this one, too. The chicken, however, instantly thought the arrangement had lots of charm. He snuggled down among the kittens when they slept and stood guard on the mother's head when they nursed. He didn't much like baths with her sandpaper tongue, but she was bigger than he was and could hold him down to administer one regardless of his objections.

He did have some inborn habits that disconcerted her. When she got out of the box, she expected to leave her babies behind, but the chicken had no intention of missing out on anything. When he was small, he couldn't do much about it—only yeep indignantly until she returned; when he grew a little more, much to her great surprise and consternation, he followed her.

Occasionally, he would see a dark spot on her fur, and chicken-like, he'd give it a few experimental pecks. Naturally, she did not appreciate that very much. He got away with it a few times. After that, she'd swat him solidly; if that failed to quell the pecking, she'd lie on him.

But a chicken is a chicken and a cat is a cat, and in their relationship, they developed irreconcilable differences. The very essences of their natures were at odds with one another. As a full-grown rooster, he still wanted to roost on her head, but she took issue with his standing between her ears, crowing and flapping. She wanted him to settle down and hunt for mice; he felt ruling the barnyard and crowing to make the sun come up was more important.

In this little family, like so many others, there were basic differences that made peace difficult. No one was to blame: The chicken and cat were acting on their God-given instincts. The cat wasn't wrong for acting like a cat; the rooster wasn't wrong for acting like a rooster. They each had a different view of the world and the parts they were to play.

In your family, workplace, or church, you may not see eye-to-eye with others. You may have different priorities than your mate or coworkers. You see things differently than others. For example, in your church, you may feel the children's ministry is far more important than the praise team. Does that make the others wrong? Or is it you who are wrong? Or has God made you a rooster and the others cats?

Paul described this situation as being like a body that has many parts, each with different functions. An eye isn't expected to taste or smell; it is expected to see. An ear isn't built to chew, speak, or sing; it is expected to hear. One person's strengths and capacities are meant to be appreciated and to complement another person's, and vice versa.

Unlike animals, we can think through these differences and rejoice and celebrate them. We can join and cooperate with people who have other gifts, thus finding compensation for our weaknesses and uses for our strengths, and incidentally, a beneficial and peaceful arrangement. What happened to the mother cat and the rooster? He grew into a thoroughly nasty little creature. True to form, he browbeat everything in the barnyard—except the mother cat. If he got saucy with her, she knocked him down and lay on him until he clucked, "Uncle!" If she thought he needed grooming, she still gave him a spit bath. He could be a rooster all he desired, but she was, after all, still a cat.

Don't you know that you yourselves are God's temple and that God's Spirit lives in you? If anyone destroys God's temple, God will destroy him; for God's temple is sacred, and you are that temple.

1 CORINTHIANS 3:16–17 NIV

To Paul, the Church was the very temple of God because it was the structure in which the Spirit of God dwelt. But if we introduce division and contention into the communion of the Church, we destroy the temple of God in two ways:

1. We make it impossible for the Holy Spirit to operate. As quickly as bitterness enters a church, love dries up. The truth of God cannot be seeded, cultivated, or bear fruit in the acrid atmosphere of bitterness. "Where love is, God is," but where hatred and strife are, Jesus stands at the door and knocks and knocks and knocks with no answer, no entry, and no communion. The motto of the Church is "Behold, how they love one another!" Whoever destroys that love, destroys the Church, and thereby, the temple of God.

2. We split up the Church and reduce it to ruins. No building can firmly stand if the foundations are kicked out, and the greatest weakness in the Church is the cracks in our unity. Paul pins down the root of the fractures to the worship of intellectual, worldly wisdom. It judges the worth of the message by the expertise of the delivery rather than by the truth of the message. It looks at the appearance and talent of the messenger rather than the content of the message.

Peace and unity in the Church are achieved in two ways:

1. Keeping the Cross in focus. When we gaze at the love, sacrifice, devotion, humility, and peace displayed by Jesus on the cross, pride, selfishness, and bitterness are extinguished. We cannot think of ourselves as worthy when we remember what Christ did for us.

2. Keeping the goal in focus: What is the goal of the Church? To build up one another in the nurture an admonition of the Lord. To work out our own salvation with fear and trembling. To love one another as Christ has loved the Church and has given His life for her.

For God is not
the author of confusion,
but of peace,
as in all churches of the saints.

1 CORINTHIANS 14:33

Peace in the Church—A Fruit of Many Flavors

My husband and I were mere newlyweds when we felt the call of God to travel full-time with an evangelist as musicians for his various meetings and services. Although we both were reared in the church, we were green as grass when it came to the business of professional evangelism, but everyone was kind and helpful, and many acted as mentors to us. We found ourselves singing in churches in a variety of denominations, from the very liturgical to the spontaneous, with everything in between.

Very early into our career, we were sent to a church in the coal-mining region of southern Tennessee, a church whose worship style can best be described as casual. The church doors stood open to admit worshipers who weren't fussy about when the services started or ended; nor did they mind summer breezes, stray dogs, or bees. The women wore their hair and sleeves modestly long, but they chewed tobacco and smoked like chimneys. Ashtrays were a complement to the salt and pepper shakers on the tables in the fellowship hall, and a spittoon stood in every corner.

This was a radical departure from the churches where my husband and I were reared, but what really threw us for a loop was the music. The songs were played by an ensemble, conducted by the preacher's wife who played the organ at the same time with the enthusiasm of a roller rink accompanist.

Picking and strumming with her was her tall, lanky brother—the county bluegrass banjo picker—and another man who played a very lively electric bass. Every song, whether it was "Marching to Zion" or "The Old Rugged Cross" had precisely the same tempo—fast! Although my husband and I played contemporary Christian folk music, they probably thought we were very staid by comparison!

Then, during the Sunday morning service, the preacher's wife spontaneously declared that the congregation was going to have a Jericho march. My husband and I looked at one another with puzzlement. In our long years of going to church, neither of us had any idea how such a thing was accomplished—at least not without a walled city and ram's horn. We soon discovered, however, that a Jericho march could very well be accomplished by the entire congregation promenading around the church building, led by the preacher's wife, my husband, and me, while she carried the Christian, United States, and Confederate flags.

Midway through the first lap, with the congregation enthusiastically singing "When the Saints Go Marching In," we somehow managed to hear the telephone ring. The preacher's wife handed the flags to my husband and said, "Here, Brother John, you lead this Jericho march!" and off she went to answer the phone.

We still didn't have the faintest idea what was supposed to

happen next. Were we supposed to march around the church seven times, then give a mighty shout while the banjo player picked an A-flat chord? My husband and I still laugh about the bewildered expressions on each other's faces as we held the flags and wondered what to do, while the expectant crowd waited behind us. Uncertain of the protocol, we marched the congregation back to their seats in what may have been the shortest Jericho march in that church's history!

In our travels, we came across devoted Christian believers who had a wide variety of practices as well as some who made doctrinal issues out of minutia. There were groups who believed a woman shouldn't shave her legs while some didn't understand why hygiene should be an issue at all. Others thought women shouldn't speak in public while some churches were founded and pastored by women. Some believed a Christian believer shouldn't wear contacts or glasses but trust God for healing. Others didn't believe healing still occurred in the present.

But regardless of whether the service structure was formal or unceremonious, whether the congregation practiced Jericho marches, foot washing, hand clapping, or long Quaker silences, one truth united all the churches we visited: Jesus Christ, the only begotten Son of God, was crucified, risen, and soon returning.

When in eternity God judges our lives, the question He

will ask us is this: "Did you follow the Prince of Peace? Did He reign in your heart? Did He reign in your church?" Our ability to follow Him will be the only thing that truly matters then, either to us or to God. Our other differences will be totally unimportant.

Praying for Peace in the Church

Finally, brothers. . . Aim for perfection, listen to my appeal, be of one mind, live in peace. And the God of love and peace will be with you. 2 CORINTHIANS 13:11 NIV

One of the best ways
of making peace with our enemies
is to pray for them,
for no one can hate a man
and pray for him
at the same time.

WILLIAM BARCLAY

Weeding the Soul on Our Knees

The two ladies had hated each other so long that neither could remember what their feud was originally all about. Each blamed the other, and each claimed that she would be willing to bury the hatchet somewhere else besides in the other woman's back, but since her adversary wouldn't, she wasn't about to leave herself unprotected.

The ladies had never actually come to blows, but the preacher's wife, Jane, sometimes was afraid they would.

"They would get so angry with one another! Their faces would turn red, and one or the other would end up stamping out of a service. They were pulling the church apart."

After much prayer, Jane approached each woman separately and asked if she would be willing to pray for the other.

"I think they were surprised at my question, but they both agreed. However, I still didn't feel at peace about the situation. It was like the Lord was nudging me to get the two of them together."

Jane asked both women to meet with her at church on a hot afternoon in July. The front door of the church was thrown open to receive the breeze, but the atmosphere inside the building was sticky and tense. Both women were the very picture of wounded dignity, and it was obvious to Jane that they were still angry.

Said Jane: "I asked each of them for her car keys and I put them in my pocket. Then I knelt down at the front pew and said to the ladies, 'I want you to kneel here with me and pray for each other. We're going to stay here as long as it takes to get this resolved!'

"I started praying out loud for each woman, and they were sort of glaring at one another over my back. Finally, one lady knelt down and started to pray for the other. I looked up and said to the woman who was standing, 'Kneel down!' She just scowled at me, so I said to her again, 'You're not going anywhere so you might as well kneel down here.' "

Jane said that the woman reluctantly knelt, but as she heard the woman on the other side of Jane praying for her, she began to weep uncontrollably. Before long, they were in each other's arms begging for forgiveness.

"I wouldn't have arranged the meeting if I hadn't known it was something God wanted, but I know God wants us to live at peace with one another and to have peace within the Church."

Like a River Glorious

Like a river glorious is God's perfect peace,
Over all victorious in its bright increase;
Perfect, yet it floweth fuller every day,
Perfect, yet it groweth deeper all the way.

Hidden in the hollow of His blessed hand,
Never foe can follow, Never traitor stand;
Not a surge of worry, not a shade of care,
Not a blast of hurry touch the spirit there.

Every joy or testing comes from God above,
Given to His children as an act of love;
We may trust Him fully all for us to do—
Those who trust Him wholly find Him wholly true.

Trusting in Jehovah,
Hearts are fully blest—
Finding, as He promised,
Perfect peace and rest.

The Fruit of Perfect Peace

In 1944, as a young man new to the pastorate, Charlie was assigned to a small, obscure country church that was not exactly in the middle of nowhere—but he said it had the same zip code! He served in this humble setting for approximately four years, garnering the well-wishes and kindly thoughts of his fellow ministers.

About that time, the leaders of the denomination decided the pastors needed a superintendent to visit the churches, encourage the pastors, and keep them informed as to what was going on all over the state. Because there was some animosity and jealousy among the leaders and because Charlie had good relationships with all of the opposing parties, he was elected to the position of superintendent. He attacked the job at hand with enthusiasm, and although most of the pastors under him had far more education and experience, he tried to pull together the farthest flung factions of the denomination.

Some of the older pastors were indignant that a young man was inquiring into their churches' business. They felt they should have been considered for such a high-profile position before a man with only four years' experience. To top it off, the bad blood among the executives also spilled over onto Charlie. "I didn't appreciate the jealousy—nor did I particularly enjoy the job," said Charlie.

Committing his way to the Lord, Charlie decided to make a change. "At the next conference (where pastors were assigned churches), I applied for any church needing a pastor that none of the other preachers wanted," he said. In making that decision, he went from the most plum position in the denomination to the lowliest, as he was assigned a church that was the laughingstock of both the town and the other pastors.

"This church had only seven active church members—all elderly—and they were fighting amongst themselves," said Charlie. For this, he was awarded the princely wage of $700 a year and a dilapidated parsonage that had been rented to strangers and further abused. Mediating the battles among the seven elderly church members was no easy task, and Charlie didn't consider them fertile ground for growing his new church.

However, the Rural Electrification Act opened up possibilities for him. "I was skilled in electrical wiring," Charlie said, "and power lines were being extended into the countryside at that time. I managed to mix the electrical wiring of farms, churches, and rural schools with my ministry. The work gave me peace of mind, income, and contact with many unchurched people. I made a peaceful living, and my ministry was enhanced by many of my customers coming to the church I served."

Soon, Charlie's church was larger than all three of the other churches in the town combined. Today, it remains one of the biggest churches in the denomination. Charlie believes God blessed his ministry because he trusted in Him, not in position or power. "Peace, position, prosperity, and power come from submitting to God," said Charlie. "He sometimes lets us go through troubled times to help us sort out our priorities, but if we remain faithful to Him through whatever, He delivers us. That is why I have always felt God's peace in my ministry."

If any of you has a dispute with another, dare he take it before the ungodly for judgment instead of before the saints? Do you not know that the saints will judge the world? And if you are to judge the world, are you not competent to judge trivial cases? . . . Therefore, if you have disputes about such matters, appoint as judges even men of little account in the church! . . . Is it possible that there is nobody among you wise enough to judge a dispute between believers? But instead, one brother goes to law against another—and this in front of unbelievers!

The very fact that you have lawsuits among you means you have been completely defeated already. Why not rather be wronged? Why not rather be cheated? Instead, you yourselves cheat and do wrong, and you do this to your brothers.

Selected portions of
1 CORINTHIANS 6:1–2, 5–8 NIV

Digging Deeper

Typically, the Jews did not go to courts of law, but settled matters among themselves. However, the way the Greeks handled disputes was another matter! Points of law and litigation were entertainment for them. Now part of the church, the Body of Christ, and worshiping side by side, the two opposing cultures and points of view were fertile ground for division, factionalism, and trouble.

Paul's questions in 1 Corinthians 6 were pointed: Why would citizens of the Kingdom of God look for a righteous decision among the heathen? And why would one part of the body hurt another and turn to an outside source for healing? Paul's answer to those questions is hard to hear with our earthly ears: Believers should be able to thwart petty squabbles. A true follower of Christ will bear hurt herself rather than inflict it upon another. This is the answer to bringing peace and unity within the Church.

The Fruit of Peace

When Sarah was hired as Christian education director for a large, prosperous church on the edge of the inner city, she naively imagined that her plans to reach out to street children would be greeted with enthusiasm.

"Each time I came to the church during the interview process," said Sarah, "I would see these little kids playing on the walkways and in the streets near the church, and it was like the Lord said to me, 'See those kids. Those are My precious lambs, and you are My shepherd. Go get 'em, round them up, and bring them in!' It wasn't the church kids who took my heart. While I cared about them, I wanted to reach the neighborhood kids from the projects and ghetto."

Her first assignment was to organize a midweek activity for the church children aged two through sixth grade. "This was a badly neglected program, and only about ten or twelve kids came out of a possible sixty," said Sarah. "They did a coloring page every week and waded through a very dry booklet about missions. I thought, *Missions are exciting! Let's learn about some real missions here and reach the street kids!*

"So I dropped the coloring page for the older kids and reorganized the activity to include electives such as candy making, cooking, martial arts, basketball, woodworking, painting, model rocket making, and so on. For the lesson time, I told the kids continued stories about true missionaries: Hudson Taylor, Jim Elliot, Nate Saint, and the like—ones that are absolutely thrilling sagas of courage and faith. We memorized Bible verses using all kinds of games, offered a healthy snack, and the attendance mushroomed!" Within a few weeks, the numbers swelled to over one hundred and fifty with most of the new attendees being unchurched street kids.

"It's true; most of them didn't know how to behave in church. They were exuberant, lively, and pretty undisciplined, but they were excited about God! Some of the parents started to come to midweek and Sunday worship—but this made a lot of people uncomfortable. There were so many of them coming that they nearly outnumbered the regular church people."

Sarah had scarcely been on staff for six months when she found herself the target of a great deal of criticism. "I was just amazed! I heard all kinds of wild tales about myself, and if any of them had been true, I'd have wanted me fired, too. But the worst was that some church members wanted the midweek outreach stopped. They said the kids were tearing up the church, and they weren't the kind of people they wanted to attract as new members."

At first, Sarah was stunned by this faultfinding. When it continued, she found herself getting discouraged. "About this time, I really could have lost my way, but the Lord reminded me, 'Hey, they crucified Me, too!' So I decided to get even: I prayed for my enemies!" Sarah said that she prayed God would open the eyes of her detractors to what He was doing with these street kids and would give these people a burden of love for the children. To prevent them from being a stumbling block to the little lambs, Sarah prayed that if they refused to yield to the Holy Spirit, God would move them out of the church. "Now that I look back on it, it was a bold, almost arrogant prayer, but I was fighting for the souls of the lost, and I felt strongly impressed to pray like that," said Sarah.

What happened next Sarah regards as something of a miracle. "Something really amazing happened. One of the men who had been such a vocal opponent of mine was in charge of the announcements one Sunday morning. He read the announcement about activities for midweek, and in the middle of the announcement he stopped and said, 'I've been against what was going on for the children during midweek, and I even started watching what was going on so I could file a formal complaint, but what I've seen changed my mind.' He went on to give the midweek program a glowing recommendation, then asked the congregation to have a special prayer of blessing right then for me!"

Sarah still has critics, but she tries to pray for them. "Jesus said to pray for our enemies and so I do, and I'm continually surprised at what God does. I consider God my Protector and my Defender. I just try to be obedient. I depend on Him to supply the peace in any situation."

Meditate upon these things;
give thyself wholly to them. . . .

1 TIMOTHY 4:15

Cultivating Peace among Thorns

Tears of sorrow came to Aunt Minnie's eyes when she thought of her children—not actually born from her body, but adopted by her when they were motherless little tykes. In the mid-1930s, if a farmer didn't have a wife, it was an enormous concern. So when Aunt Minnie saw the problems her brother was having with his eight very young children following the death of his wife, she completely put her life on hold and stepped into her deceased sister-in-law's shoes as mother to the children.

A pretty, sweet-faced woman from a wealthy family, Minnie had suitors aplenty, but family responsibilities came first. Aunt Minnie's youth and adulthood passed by as she washed, ironed, and cooked for her young nieces and nephews, assuming as much of the mother's role as they would permit. Above all, she took them to church, modeling the gospel message in her daily life, and she felt privileged to see each of the eight make a profession of faith and join the small local church.

One by one, they married, began their own families, and she began to feel her life slow down. Then their father, Aunt Minnie's brother, dropped dead of a sudden heart attack. In his will, he deeded his various farms, acreage, and bank accounts to Minnie, knowing she would shrewdly manage his accumulated wealth and pass it on with interest to his offspring. She didn't expect to live too long, either. After all, she was one of the oldest and the sole survivor of her many siblings.

As the family grew, the nieces and nephews began to chafe about Aunt Minnie's large holdings. She recognized the demands of the young families. So after discussion with her attorney, who was vehemently against her plan, she divided the farms and money among the eight children, holding back a fair sum for herself, just in case by some miracle of genetics she had an old age. The deal was this: The nieces and nephews could have the farms and money now, but if she ever needed the money, they would have to equally cough it up. No one ever expected to. Like Minnie, they thought she'd die pretty soon.

Turned out, though, that dying for Minnie was as hard as living. She didn't suddenly drop dead of a heart attack like the rest of her family; rather, she disappeared a tiny fragment at a time from osteoporosis. She lost height, her spine curving and weakening until she lay with her head permanently on her knees, and required twenty-four-hour nursing. Aunt Minnie wanted to go home to heaven; she wanted to be free of pain and infirmity.

But the worst hurt was that some of her nieces, nephews, and their mates wished her dead when she paid out all of her reserve and had to ask them for financial help. Not all of them resented her request, but those who did protested vociferously. "We ought to throw you out on the highway and let the trucks run over you!" one shouted when Minnie told her she needed some of the money back. This nephew and his wife flatly refused to contribute, and some of the others were equally as reluctant.

Because all of the nieces and nephews went to the same church, the rancor spilled over into the congregation. The family divided and so did the church. Several family members came to their pastor seeking guidance. "Those who are withholding money from Aunt Minnie are clearly wrong," the pastor told them. He accompanied a delegation to talk with their recalcitrant family members.

Entrenched in their position and unwilling to relinquish a dime, the opposing faction issued a challenge: "Sue us!" The others were angry enough at their miserly attitude to consider it. With a heavy heart, the pastor pointed out the sixth chapter of First Corinthians. "You certainly have legal grounds to sue your brothers and sisters," he told them, "but it will further divide your family and the church. What the Bible seems to say is that it is better if you bear the offense than if you sue a brother or sister in Christ. This is not the wisdom of the world, but the wisdom of God."

After discussing the issue at length, the willing members of the family decided to bear the offense rather than bring a lawsuit and split the church. They determined to shoulder Aunt Minnie's expenses themselves.

Aunt Minnie didn't live long after that. The sorrow of betrayal shortened her life. The church did not split, but others within the congregation and community, honest people, were wary of doing business with the stingy faction of the family. If that group would cheat their own aged aunt and kinfolk, no telling what they would do to others. Not surprisingly, the giving side found many people eager to work with and for them, knowing that these were honorable, well-meaning people.

This was an unexpected bonus, for they were not looking to lay up their reward here but in heaven. These loving people were the meek, the peacemakers, who inherited the earth—and were called the children of God and Aunt Minnie.

We cannot produce peace in our church—just as we cannot produce it in our families or even our own hearts. But as we remain joined to the vine of Christ, His Spirit will cultivate a rich and eternal harvest of peace, one that will spread from our hearts to the world around us.

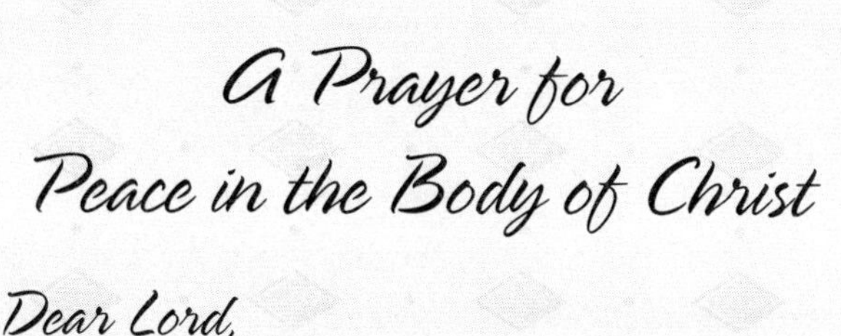

A Prayer for Peace in the Body of Christ

Dear Lord,

Help our church to aim for the mind of Christ, to be of one mind, and to live in peace. Reveal Yourself to us as the God of love and peace. Help the church to walk worthy of the vocation wherewith we are called—to be sons and daughters of God in Christ—with all lowliness and meekness,

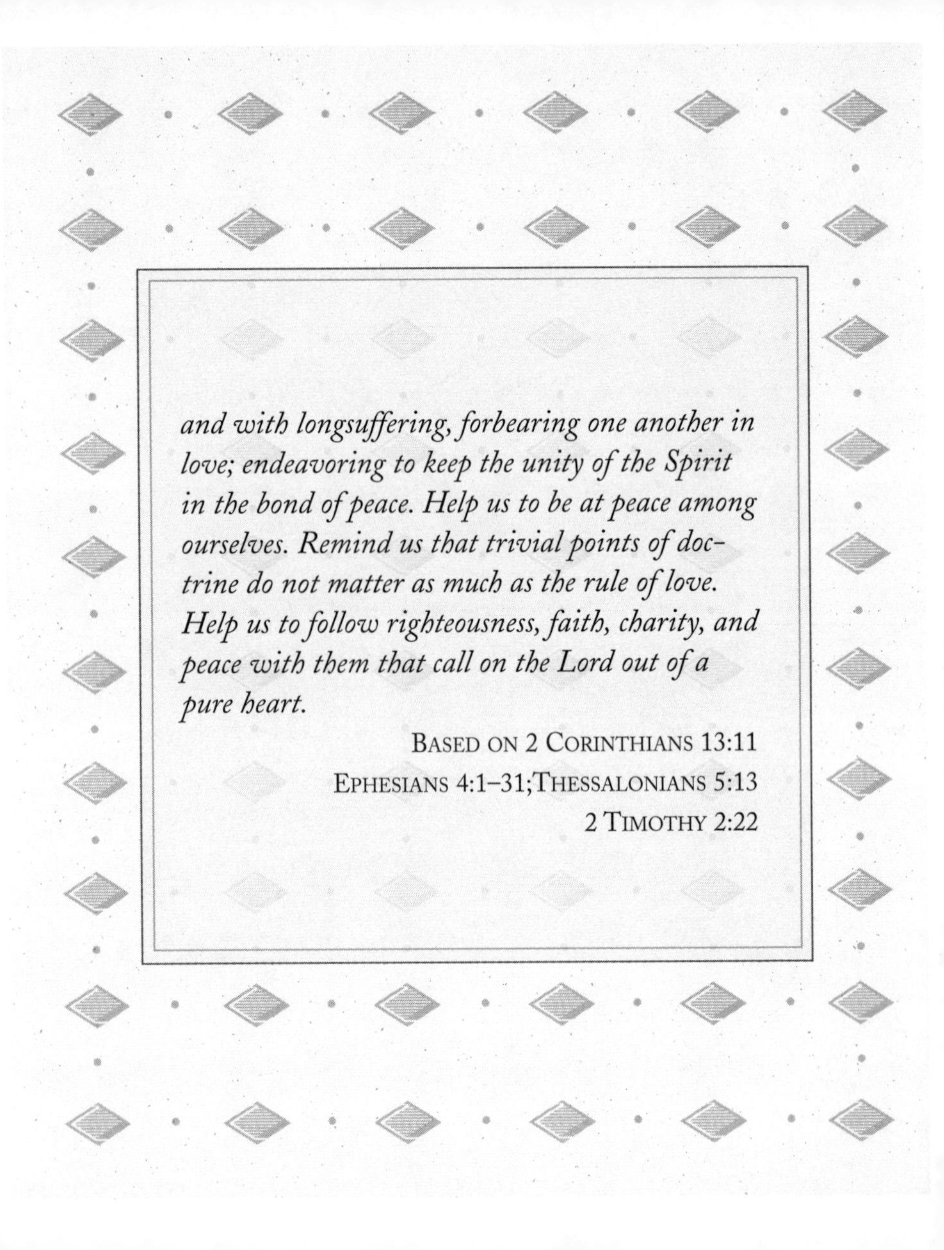

and with longsuffering, forbearing one another in love; endeavoring to keep the unity of the Spirit in the bond of peace. Help us to be at peace among ourselves. Remind us that trivial points of doctrine do not matter as much as the rule of love. Help us to follow righteousness, faith, charity, and peace with them that call on the Lord out of a pure heart.

BASED ON 2 CORINTHIANS 13:11
EPHESIANS 4:1–31; THESSALONIANS 5:13
2 TIMOTHY 2:22

The ABC's of Peace

A *Acquaint now thyself with him, and be at peace: thereby good shall come unto thee.* JOB 22:21

B *But the meek shall inherit the earth; and shall delight themselves in the abundance of peace.* PSALM 37:11

C *The* LORD *lift up his countenance upon thee, and give thee peace.* NUMBERS 6:26

D *Dominion and fear are with him, he maketh peace in his high places.* JOB 25:2

E *Depart from evil, and do good; seek peace, and pursue it.* PSALM 34:14

F *For thou shalt be in league with the stones of the field: and the beasts of the field shall be at peace with thee.* JOB 5:23

G *Go in peace: before the* LORD *is your way wherein ye go.* JUDGES 18:6

H *Hear my prayer, O* LORD, *and give ear unto my cry; hold not thy peace at my tears: for I am a stranger with thee, and a sojourner, as all my fathers were.* PSALM 39:12

I *I will both lay me down in peace, and sleep: for thou, LORD, only makest me dwell in safety.* PSALM 4:8

J *The way of peace they know not; and there is no judgment in their goings: they have made them crooked paths: whosoever goeth therein shall not know peace.* ISAIAH 59:8

K *Thou wilt keep him in perfect peace, whose mind is stayed on thee: because he trusteth in thee.* ISAIAH 26:3

L *The LORD shall fight for you, and ye shall hold your peace.* EXODUS 14:14

M *Mark the perfect man, and behold the upright: for the end of that man is peace.* PSALM 37:37

N *Think not that I am come to send peace on earth: I came not to send peace, but a sword.* MATTHEW 10:34

O *Of the increase of his government and peace there shall be no end, upon the throne of David, and upon his kingdom, to order it, and to establish it with judgment and with justice from henceforth even for ever. The zeal of the LORD of hosts will perform this.* ISAIAH 9:7

P *Pray for the peace of Jerusalem: they shall prosper that love thee. Peace be within thy walls, and prosperity within thy palaces.* PSALM 122:6–7

Q Quietness of heart: *Peace I leave with you, my peace I give unto you: not as the world giveth, give I unto you. Let not your heart be troubled, neither let it be afraid.* JOHN 14:27

R *And the work of righteousness shall be peace; and the effect of righteousness quietness and assurance for ever.*

ISAIAH 32:17

S *The LORD will give strength unto his people; the LORD will bless his people with peace.* PSALM 29:11

T *Mercy and truth are met together; righteousness and peace have kissed each other.* PSALM 85:10

U *But upon David, and upon his seed, and upon his house, and upon his throne, shall there be peace for ever from the LORD.* 1 KINGS 2:33

V *Behold, their valiant ones shall cry without: the ambassadors of peace shall weep bitterly.* ISAIAH 33:7

W *When a man's ways please the* L*ORD*, *he maketh even his enemies to be at peace with him.* PROVERBS 16:7

X *For thus saith the* L*ORD*, *Behold, I will extend peace to her like a river, and the glory of the Gentiles like a flowing stream. . . .* ISAIAH 66:12

Y *Yea, thou shalt see thy children's children, and peace upon Israel.* PSALM 128:6

Z *For Zion's sake will I not hold my peace, and for Jerusalem's sake I will not rest, until the righteousness thereof go forth as brightness, and the salvation thereof as a lamp that burneth.* ISAIAH 62:1

Make Us Worthy, Lord

Make us worthy, Lord,
To serve our fellow men throughout the world
Who live and die in poverty and hunger.
Give them, through our hands, this day
Their daily bread, and by our understanding love give
Peace and joy.
Lord, make me a channel of Thy peace,
That where there is hatred I may bring love;
That where there is wrong, I may bring the spirit of
  forgiveness;
That where there is doubt, I may bring faith;
That where there is error, I may bring truth;

That where there is discord, I may bring harmony;
That where there is despair, I may bring hope;
That where there are shadows, I may bring light;
That where there is sadness, I may bring joy;

Lord, grant that I may seek to comfort rather than to
    be comforted;
To understand rather than to be understood;
To love rather than to be loved;
For it is by forgetting self that one finds;
It is by dying that one awakens to eternal life.
Amen.

MOTHER TERESA

About the Author

Rebekah Montgomery has over thirty years of experience as a children's pastor and teacher. A prolific writer, she is the author of several books; many magazine, newspaper, and inspirational articles; camp and Bible school curriculum; and children's musicals. Rebekah is the author of *Ordinary Miracles: True Stories of an Extraordinary God Who Works in Our Everyday Lives* (Promise Press, May 2000), and is presently developing a book series on the fruit of the Spirit (Promise Press, July 2000).

Rebekah lives in Kewanee, Illinois, with John, her husband of thirty years, and their three children, Mary, Joel, and Daniel.